New Graduate's Guide to Physiotherapy

Avoid burnout and injury, build resilience and thrive in clinical practice

Elizabeth Santos

Physiotherapist

First published by Busybird Publishing 2019

Copyright © 2019 Elizabeth Santos

ISBN
Print: 978-1-925949-92-6
Ebook: 978-1-925949-33-9

Elizabeth Santos has asserted her right under the Copyright, Designs and Patents Act 1988 to be identified as the author of this work. The information in this book is based on the author's experiences and opinions. The publisher specifically disclaims responsibility for any adverse consequences, which may result from use of the information contained herein. Permission to use information has been sought by the author. Any breaches will be rectified in further editions of the book.

All rights reserved. No part of this publication may be reproduced, stored in or introduced into a retrieval system, or transmitted in any form, or by any means (electronic, mechanical, photocopying, recording or otherwise) without the prior written permission of the author. Any person who does any unauthorised act in relation to this publication may be liable to criminal prosecution and civil claims for damages. Enquiries should be made through the publisher.

Cover image: Busybird Publishing

Cover design: Busybird Publishing

Layout and typesetting: Busybird Publishing

Busybird Publishing
2/118 Para Road
Montmorency, Victoria
Australia 3094
www.busybird.com.au

*To the new graduate physiotherapist with a
hopeful heart and a spring in their step.*

Contents

Praise	1
Acknowledgements	3
Foreword	5
Introduction - My Story	7
The Call to Adventure	**9**
1 - Finding a Job	9
2 - The First Years in Clinical Practice	14
3 - Primary Areas of Practice	18
4 - Continuing Professional Development and Career Pathways	28
Working with Others	**33**
5 - The Therapeutic Relationship	33
6 - Mentoring	42
7 - Team Relationships Within the Workplace	47
8 - Multi-disciplinary Approaches and Referrals	53
9 - Clinical Reasoning, Evidence-based Practice and Outcome Measurement Tools	58
10 - Working with Compensable Clients and Third Parties	63
Challenges on the Path	**68**
11 - Perfectionism, Over-commitment and the High Achiever	68
12 - Professionalism, Social Media and Confidentiality	73
13 - Informed Consent, Documentation and Medico-legal Matters	79
14 - Remuneration, Contracts and Leave Entitlements	86
15 - Grief and Loss	93
Burnout and Injury	**96**
16 - Why do Physiotherapists Burn Out?	96
17 - Why do Physiotherapists Become Injured?	104
18 - Retention: Why do Some Physiotherapists Leave the Profession?	108
The Future Looks Bright: A Progressive Profession	**112**
19 - Extended/Advanced Scope of Practice and Technological Advancements	112
20 - Physiotherapist as Coach: Goal-setting with Clients	116
21 - Holistic and Integrative Approaches	122
Caring for the Self and Others	**128**
22 - Mindfulness for Physiotherapists	128
23 - Building Resilience	132
24 - Self-care for Physiotherapists	135
25 - Community Care and Philanthropy	140
Afterword	**144**
The Journey	144
Connect with Elizabeth	145
About the Author	146
Bibliography	148

Praise

This book is a great start for final year physiotherapy students! It covers the nitty gritty things that are beyond clinical practice alone, teaching the reader how to be a good physiotherapist as a whole. Overall, definitely a great read.

                                                                  Z.N., recent graduate

The most valuable part of the book for me was the section covering burnout; how to recognise it and prevent it occurring. I had not heard of an outcome measure for burnout (such as the MBI) and found it very helpful and have kept it for future use. It also may help me recognise it in workmates and potentially make a difference in their lives and career.

                                                                   H.R., recent graduate

This book is exactly what students need in their final year of the physiotherapy degree. It provides much-needed clarity regarding what the first few years of practice may look like, and how to avoid burnout in the future. Would highly recommend this book to fellow students also seeking guidance on their future physiotherapy career!

                                    Jessica Gourlay, physiotherapy student

Elizabeth has combined her wealth of experience with practical and well-researched advice for any new graduate looking to establish a sustainable physiotherapy career. Her clear passion for patient-centred, holistic healthcare shines through in this insightful and encouraging guide. It deserves a place on every student's bookshelf.

                                                                   J.H., recent graduate

There are many things to juggle as a physiotherapist and Elizabeth frames the need to reflect, prioritise and strive for wellbeing for the self (and others) in such a tangible way. She captures the broad scope of physiotherapy practice with clarity and encouragement for new graduates, ultimately setting them up for a rewarding career. This is a book I wish I had in my early years of practice.

                                  Amanda Sadauskas, Shift Physiotherapy

A wonderfully well-researched primer for the new physiotherapist to help get their head around all that the profession can offer, and how they may best fit within these systems. Lots of practical guidance for self-reflection to help the novice make good decisions early on in their career.

Tory Toogood, Vital Core Physiotherapy

This book helps the new graduate and holds their hand whilst allowing them to find their own way in the real working world. It looks at common difficulties and how you can either prepare for them or (preferably) prevent them. I particularly like the section on perfectionism, which is a trait most physiotherapists have. I have learnt over the past 20 years of practice that 'progression' not 'perfection' is a far better way to go. It would have been nice as a new graduate to have had that pointed out to me.

Rebecca Sabine, Vital Core Physiotherapy

Acknowledgements

Thank you to my parents, siblings, aunties, in-laws, and extended family for your encouragement throughout the process of writing, editing and publishing – I love you all and care for you deeply. Thank you Ricardo, my love, my life. Without your support and help to care for our beautiful boy Leonardo (so mummy could write) this book would not have been written.

A special thank you to my twin brother, Dr Andrew McLean, I'm grateful for your unending faith in me and for your academically minded guidance with the direction of this work.

There are many inspirational practitioners that have greatly influenced my path and I wish to thank them here. Thanks go to Tara-Ellen Schebella and Dr David Spurrier for your physiotherapy treatment, and for reigniting my faith in myself and in physiotherapy after I sustained a back injury as a new graduate. I'd also like to thank Ayurvedic practitioner, naturopath and herbalist Kester Marshall, psychologist Annette Berwald, chiropractors Dr Maria Coote and Dr Amanda Chow for their roles in my healing.

Thank you to my previous employers and mentors, Kylie Brammy, Janie Jenkins and Jane Brammy, for your generosity of spirit and influential role in my career, and to the amazing former team at Therapia Physiotherapy and Pilates – I have happy memories of my time there and am so pleased we still keep in touch.

I also wish to thank other previous colleagues including Dr Susie Thomas, Professor Maria Crotty, Adam Govier, Lauren Locke, Andrea Koch, Gabrielle Packham, Melissa Connell, Julie Crook, Haydn Gambling and Karen Custance for being good role models and support people. Thank you to additional mentors and inspirational teachers, in no particular order, including Cameron Brown, Kiarna Ella, Deborah Chalk, Cassie Mendoza-Jones, Monique Alamedine, Adam Gibson, David Stellfox, Marni LeFevre, Jane Copeland, Corona Brady, Natasa Denman, Kelly Notaras, Tim Grahl, Marcus Bird, Robert Medhurst, Ken King, Tracey Cooke and Nicky Baker.

Thank you to my dear loyal friends who believed in me and asked me about the book – you know who you are. Thank you to my godparents, Jo and David Mercer, for teaching me that service to community is the most important thing.

Thank you to Rebecca Sabine and Tory Toogood and the wonderful team at Vital Core Physiotherapy for the positivity, camaraderie and for always encouraging further personal and professional development.

Thank you to the experienced physiotherapists and recent graduates whom I spoke with over the years that this book came to light, to find out why physiotherapy as a profession can be so marvellous, yet so challenging at times too.

Thank you to Kris Franken for your copy-editing support with cover text and 'About the Author', and to Erin McWhinney for copy-editing the manuscript so skilfully. Thank you to Sonia Cortez for styling and Margarita Ceko for author photography.

Thank you to Busybird Publishing for all of your help and effort to make this dream come to life, with special thanks to Blaise van Hecke and Kev Howlett for managing the project, cover design and formatting. Thank you Megan Hills for your gorgeous and hilarious drawings that have added humour and lightness to a somewhat serious topic. Thank you to everyone who helped make this book happen and thank you to the readers (especially the enthusiastic early beta readers) for your interest in these ideas.

Foreword

It's with great pleasure and gratitude that I introduce readers to this informative book. When Liz first started this book, I, as a manual therapy instructor and mentor to many young physiotherapists, thought it was much needed and timely. Seven years later, upon its completion, the information contained within this book is required reading for all recent graduates.

Over the thirty-year span of my own physiotherapy career, I've witnessed significant changes within the profession, including a sevenfold increase in Australia's annual graduate numbers, corporatisation of the industry and a distinct departure from its manual therapy roots. With change comes opportunities, challenges and consequences. In this well-sequenced and thoroughly researched book, Liz meticulously explores the challenges facing new graduates and the opportunities that await them now and into the future. The consequences of high rates of practitioner injury, burnout and career attrition, particularly among younger therapists, are highlighted, and practical suggestions and solutions are outlined. As with any problem, diagnosing the underlying contributing factors and addressing the causes – not just the symptoms – are key to a successful outcome.

The early years of any career are filled with much excitement and aspiration, mixed with many moments of uncertainty, introspection and frustration. The self-enquiry encouraged at the completion of each chapter helps the reader to verify this broad range of emotions and poses further questions to ponder. In doing so, Liz has recognised that many of the answers to the new graduate's questions lie within themselves and just need to be resolved with guided reflection. Where this is still difficult, Liz has encouraged readers to seek advice from a mentor, with guidelines on how to find the person who best suits their needs.

In both the public and private sectors, there are a myriad of potential stumbling blocks for new graduates. Despite the fact that most new graduates find work in private practice, there's little room within undergraduate university curriculums to cover the practical day-to-day issues that are specific to this sector. It often takes young physiotherapists years to navigate their way through this maze, leaving little time and energy to develop their competence as practitioners. This book comprehensively addresses many of these important issues, allowing the new graduate to not only anticipate what lies ahead, but to respond in a considered manner when faced with these challenges. In this book, Liz has outlined a blueprint for therapists to not just survive the difficult first years, but to thrive as they successfully navigate their way along their desired career path.

I congratulate Liz, who has integrated her multi-faceted skill base and years of experience as a physiotherapist to create a book that will not only make an important contribution to the physiotherapy profession, but will inspire and enrich the lives of those who read it, as well as those they help to heal.

Haydn Gambling BAppScPhysio, JSCCI

Physiotherapist and Manual Therapy Instructor, Manual Therapy Institute

Adelaide, South Australia

Introduction

—

My Story

I first learned about burnout and injury in physiotherapy the hard way; through personal experience. It began in 2008, in my second year of clinical practice, when I 'caught' a falling stroke patient. I managed to save the man from hitting the floor but sustained a low back injury in the process. This incident was the beginning of a cycle of burnout and injury that would last just over five years. It took me on an epic journey across multiple roles, with many different mentors. I was frustrated and in search of answers, with this unshakeable feeling that I had missed something.

I had always practised yoga, walked regularly and, despite my small stature, felt confident in clinical practice. I knew about the inherent risks in manual handling, but always thought injury was something that happened to other people.

I decided not to make a claim through WorkCover, and instead left the hospital for a career change and went to work in research, which was light on my back and a welcome change. My disc injury slowly improved over time, although I did have exacerbations and remissions in the pins and needles and numbness in my leg and the central pain. I had treatment with some top physiotherapists in my hometown of Adelaide, Australia, and received training in the Pilates method of rehabilitation so that I could help myself and others with back pain. I discovered McKenzie techniques for reducing low back pain, improving posture and 'treating your own back'. I learned about pain and sensitisation and I sought help and wisdom from many health practitioners along the way. I went on a remarkable journey of healing which took me all over the world, meditating with monks, attending international yoga retreats and motivational conferences, and digging deep into the body, mind and soul in order to heal.

I continued to work as a physiotherapist throughout it all, and began studying a second bachelor degree to become a naturopath as well. I still struggled intermittently with back pain, but by the end of my studies I was feeling fitter, stronger and healthier than ever before. I took up meditation, drank green smoothies, went for long walks and practised yoga and Pilates. By the time I became pregnant and had my baby, I had no back pain at all. This was a huge relief because I had always wondered how I would cope with pregnancy and birthing with a 'bad back'.

As I recovered from my injury and professional burnout, I realised there must be other physiotherapists out there who had been injured, burnt out, or at some point questioned whether they should continue with physiotherapy. I started writing this book in 2012 and dived with vigour into the research on burnout and injury among physiotherapists. I spoke to physiotherapists in the field (both novices and experienced practitioners) for their insights. I also began hosting workshops in Adelaide in 2017 called 'self-care sessions' to support health professionals, helpers and carers to better identify the signs of burnout and equip them with tools and resources for self-care.

This book is designed to be read in any order that appeals to you. You can flick to any of the chapters that you feel are important. By reading this book and incorporating the self-enquiry activities into your daily routine, you can truly begin to nourish yourself as a practitioner and learn to identify the warning signs of burnout early to help prevent an acute episode. Of course, if you are already heading along the treacherous path to burnout, this book can act as a guide and wise companion, gently bringing you back from the brink with a warm hug and giving you the tools you need to find balance and truly enjoy your career as a clinician.

I know how life-changing it can be to have your career interrupted by burnout and injury, and it is my sincere wish that you avoid the discomfort and inconvenience that burnout brings and develop strategies to ensure you live your best life as a physiotherapist. I look forward to sharing the journey with you and I'm here for you when you need that little extra reassurance. May you learn to care for yourself as well as you care for others.

The Call to Adventure

1
Finding a Job

When the student is ready the teacher will appear. When the student is truly ready ... the teacher will disappear.

Lao Tzu

Readiness to Gain Employment

It's an exciting time as the new graduate nears the end of the degree and begins looking to the future. Which areas of physiotherapy practice appeal? How does one take the first steps towards seeking employment? Does the new physiotherapist actually feel ready at all? These are the important questions that new graduates must explore as they embark on the next stage of their development: finding a job.

A small research paper from the UK looked at readiness for gaining employment in physiotherapy and found that there have been changes in working in the National Health System (NHS) in the last decade, with fewer job prospects and greater competitiveness for the available positions.[1] The study used questionnaires to determine how ready graduates felt for the employment process and how prepared they were to make job applications to potential employers. Results were poor and indicated that students had difficulty identifying essential skills for employment, including prioritisation of caseload, time management and legal documentation. Overall, students had limited awareness of the application procedure and pre-interview selection criteria, which impacted their ability to make a successful application.

So how can the physiotherapist increase their understanding of these essential skills? How does a physiotherapist go about applying for jobs and seeking references, and what support is required for this process to occur?

The Application Process

When it comes to putting together a curriculum vitae (CV), one of the first things to consider is personal branding. This is the way in which an individual expresses their own story online and informs others about themselves.[2] This storytelling approach to branding has been highlighted in the research as a way to build reputation and promote one's uniqueness, which can create a competitive advantage. When businesses are looking to hire, they often want to know what kind of person they are hiring. The quality of a professional presence across online platforms can make or break an application.[3] Therefore, it is important to consider what a potential employer might find when they perform a web search for a candidate's online profiles.

While online presence is important, it is one small part of the recruitment process and what will matter more to an employer is a candidate's personality and how well they are going to fit into the team. Technical or 'hard' skills can always be learned, but soft skills, such as how one develops relationships with others (covered in Chapter 5) and how to be a team player (covered in Chapter 7), are more closely related to personality and not as easy to teach.

Meeting all of the criteria in the job description will also make a big difference to an employer seeking a thorough, highly organised candidate with attention to detail. For the candidate, it's essential to read all details of the role carefully, and ensure they address the criteria and can communicate this to the employer.

Finding a mentor, lecturer, or someone from the university support services to work with can be an excellent way to prepare an application and feel ready for an interview. And while support beforehand is incredibly beneficial, seeking help afterwards also has its benefits. A post-interview meeting is useful to debrief and discuss what could be done better next time.

Success in the job market comes with determination, perseverance and hard work. Practising clinical examples and gaining experience with challenging clients and conflict situations can help the new graduate learn and communicate these lessons to a potential employer.

Role-playing with other students or a mentor is a powerful way to practise before a job interview. Writing out (and practising aloud) answers to 'mock' questions can be helpful for increasing confidence, as can imagining oneself on stage 'performing' responses to interview questions.

Adequate communication is essential and may take many forms during the application process. It might involve a phone call to the contact person for more information about the job. It might mean speaking with last year's graduates to learn about their experiences in the role and what the benefits and challenges might be. This information can be invaluable in a job interview, as it provides insight and an edge for the graduate. Taking action in a timely manner is also important. Don't delay putting in that application. Those who apply promptly and show passion for the role will often catch the eye of the employer. Enthusiasm is contagious and may well lead to a successful outcome.

Preparedness for Practice

The promise of a new career is exciting and daunting, but just how ready for clinical practice does a new physiotherapist *actually* feel once their study is over?

"Get warmed up with these. We'll throw you in the deep end this afternoon"

A qualitative study (Atkinson & McElroy 2016) explored this question and looked specifically at new practitioner readiness for jobs in private practice. The study found that building preparedness in novice physiotherapists could involve working with sporting teams, receiving additional radiological instruction on top of what students received during their hospital placement, undertaking clinical placements in private practice, building supportive colleague relations, and professional development. The findings of the study indicate that there are many ways to bolster confidence, and the new graduate need not choose all of these but could consider one or two of the above.[4]

A similar study (Adam, Peters & Chipchase 2013) looked at the readiness of new graduates to work in the area of workplace health and safety (WHS, known as Occupational Health and Safety in Victoria and Western Australia).[5] The attributes required for competency in this area of physiotherapy were found to be communication, clinical reasoning, assessment of injury and illness management, and ethical practice. Problem-solving skills, confidence, timeliness and the ability to be flexible across situations were also of high importance.

A final Irish paper considered the readiness of final-year students from their own perspective and highlighted some key insights.[6] The students were asked to look at three themes:

1. **Aspects of their curriculum that students perceived to be supportive of their transition into primary healthcare practice**

2. **Aspects of their curriculum that students perceived to be deficient**

3. **Aspects of their curriculum that students perceived to be requiring change.**

From the first category, practice with problem-based learning was highlighted as helpful, along with interdisciplinary learning where students worked with other students to learn what other disciplines do. From the second category, looking at deficiency, there was a perceived lack of clinical placements available. Students also commented on a lack of understanding of health promotion and education and how to communicate effectively with patients and other members of the team. Thirdly, in terms of changing the curriculum, students wanted to see every student given the opportunity to have a clinical placement in a primary healthcare role to understand the administration and how to work with others in clinic and at home.

Finding a job requires a multi-faceted approach. Developing a good CV, seeking the right support to feel job-ready, having a proactive approach and following up in a timely manner are important elements. If the new graduate physiotherapist can remain self-aware, engaged, positive and confident and be persistent in their efforts, they will ultimately find the right role in that formative and very important first year as a physiotherapist.

Questions for Self-enquiry

1. Are you confident with your CV? Is it current, clear and concise?

2. Have you received one-on-one support for interview preparation and review of your CV? If not, do you have a support person or mentor to ask for help?

3. Do you know which area(s) of physiotherapy you would most like to work in? Is there a support person or mentor you could ask for help if unsure?

4. Have you sought any extra-curricular experience with sporting teams, community centres or within private practice?

5. Could you consider relevant paid or volunteer work to help broaden your experience and add to your CV, and if so, what steps could you take to arrange this?

6. What do you really desire from that first job? Flexibility? Adventure? Something else?

7. What are your strengths? What unique contribution can you make to your employer's business and the team, and how can you best express that in your CV or an interview?

2
The First Years in Clinical Practice

*Twenty years from now you will be more disappointed by the things
you didn't do than by the ones you did do. So throw off the bowlines.
Sail away from the safe harbour. Catch the trade winds in your sails.
Explore. Dream. Discover.*

Mark Twain

The formative years as a new physiotherapist are exciting, challenging, rewarding, and empowering – but professional life can be daunting too. University education does its best to prepare the student for life outside of the institution, but there will always be surprises along the way. The transition from student to practitioner requires significant growth, and the new physiotherapist will find their life changes considerably as they adapt to their new role. The days may feel longer, and there will certainly be fewer breaks as the graduate adjusts to life without university holidays.

Developing a Professional Identity

In the first year of work, new graduates must access and attempt to retain vast amounts of information on a daily basis. Some of this information relates to individual client care, but much of it is about building a new identity in a strange environment with new colleagues and work practices.

A small UK study produced some interesting qualitative data on the construction of professional identity by physiotherapists.[7] The study comprised a series of focus groups and interviews and explored the ethical dilemmas, successes and unresolved anxieties faced by these new graduates in order to better understand the formation of professional identity. The study found that professional identity is more complex than traditionally thought and depends in part on location and the community in which a physiotherapist is practising. Developing an identity is an ongoing and dynamic process in which physiotherapists have to make sense of and interpret their professional self-concept based on evolving attributes, beliefs, values and motives.

The undergraduate curriculum plays a large part in job readiness and assists with the transition into becoming part of a team – a crucial element of developing an identity as a clinician. Understanding one's role in an interdisciplinary team is incredibly important and can take time to develop in the real world. The Interprofessional Learning (IPL) framework helps new clinicians to become effective team members.[8] IPL is designed to improve socialisation between professional groups and create rewarding interactions so that physiotherapists can identify similarities between professions and form positive relationships with allied health and medical teams.

Mentoring and Support

The amount of mentoring a physiotherapist receives will depend on their role. Mentoring varies across roles and workplaces, and it is worth considering how to seek support during the formative years as a clinician. Mentoring does extend beyond those first years, but it is most important early on when the physiotherapist is being shaped and moulded. All practitioners require someone superior to teach them and guide them, no matter what age or stage they are at – there is always more to learn. Mentoring will be explored in more detail in Chapter 6.

A study looking at supervision requirements during the transition of occupational therapists into the workforce in Australia found that the process is multi-faceted, and involves unique and challenging experiences including stress, value conflict and role uncertainty (Melman et al. 2016). Because the transition is complex, supervision and support are required to help with developing key competencies and determining directions for professional development; these in turn enhance quality of care and feelings of self-efficacy.[9]

Job Satisfaction

Job satisfaction is an important part of avoiding burnout and reducing staff turnover. One paper identified factors that affect job satisfaction, including autonomy, commitment to the organisation and access to continuing professional development.[10] Perceived extreme challenge was felt to have a negative impact on satisfaction. Other issues correlating with reduced satisfaction included a lack of opportunity to perform extra duties or be promoted within an organisation, as well as poor financial incentives. The study involved an online survey of new graduates in the main clinical streams of paediatrics, aged care, musculoskeletal, cardiorespiratory and neurology.

While the choice of clinical area can influence a physiotherapist's enjoyment in their work, there are many other factors that can also affect job satisfaction. Working conditions, pay rates, caseloads, professional development opportunities (or lack thereof), holidays and perceived support must also be considered. Taking time to reflect on what is going well and what isn't going well is a proactive way for a new graduate to begin to work towards solutions. This will be covered further in Chapter 18.

Self-esteem and Developing Confidence

According to the literature, self-esteem refers to an individual's overall self-evaluation of their own competencies.[11] It has been suggested that an individual's self-esteem plays a significant role in determining motivation, work-related attitudes and behaviours. Self-esteem is normally relatively high in childhood, then drops in adolescence, rises gradually throughout adulthood, and then declines sharply in old age.[12] Employment status, household income, and satisfaction in the domains of work, relationships, and health can contribute to a more positive lifespan trajectory of self-esteem.[13]

Many (if not all) practitioners will have times in their career when they feel inadequate. While this is common for new graduates, low self-esteem can still be experienced by practitioners of all ages, and may be affected by the work environment, the quality of relationships with colleagues and the demands of the role. Older practitioners, while wiser and more experienced in patient care, may feel inadequate in contrast to a new graduate with fresh knowledge of the latest technology and techniques. Professional development and upskilling can increase practitioner competency and self-esteem at all stages of one's career.

Confidence has been defined as 'a feeling or consciousness of one's powers or of reliance on one's circumstances.'[14] Often it is *oneself* who is being relied upon, although having a solid team or support network of professionals can also help. So what does confidence in clinical practice actually look like? It may be the way a practitioner calmly but boldly introduces themselves to a new client, or the way they explain a diagnosis or treatment plan. Perhaps it involves problem-solving for a client's case, with the end result being a satisfied client and positive treatment outcomes.

Monitoring self-talk can sometimes be of benefit. Negative ideas may be leftover opinions or beliefs from others that have been taken on and internalised. Perhaps there was once criticism from an employer, a colleague, a lecturer or supervisor, a parent, partner or even a friend. Processing these past events is an important part of making peace with them and moving forward to cultivate greater confidence.

Strategies for developing confidence include:

1. **Journaling to determine negative beliefs and reframing them as positive ones**
2. **Positive affirmations and cultivating positive inner dialogue, and developing awareness of negative self-talk**
3. **Using positive body language, appropriate laughter and smiles.**

Learning to develop confidence, being aware of what can reduce self-esteem and cultivating positive inner dialogue are essential elements of success in clinical practice in the early years.

Questions for Self-enquiry

1. What are you looking forward to in your first year as a physiotherapist?
2. What professional development would you like to pursue in your first year of study?
3. Do you have support from your employer or other mentor?
4. How do you anticipate you will cope with changes to your lifestyle?
5. Do you feel confident about clinical practice?
6. What inner dialogue do you find yourself running a lot of the time? Is it mostly positive or negative? Does your inner critic tell you you're not good enough, successful enough, knowledgeable enough? Write down any negative inner dialogue so that you can reframe it in a positive way.

3
Primary Areas of Practice

To be yourself in a world that is constantly trying to make you something else is the greatest accomplishment.

Ralph Waldo Emerson

Physiotherapy as a career provides a rich array of opportunities and experiences, from private practice and sports physiotherapy to aged care, vocational rehabilitation and hospital-based roles. There is truly something for everyone.

The Public Sector

The public sector encompasses services that provide government-funded care. This varies across different regions but may extend to disability services, paediatrics and public hospitals. For acute public hospital work, the wards provide a rich learning environment and key opportunities for growth as a physiotherapist, while working as part of a larger team. It is common to commence with a rotating roster so that every twelve weeks (or other nominated time) the graduate changes to another area of clinical practice within the department. This provides excellent exposure to a wide range of clinical areas and presentations, from surgeries to unique and interesting conditions. It also affords the opportunity to learn from experienced graduates and develop skills in a supportive learning environment, particularly if it is through a teaching hospital where education is part of the framework.

There are, however, negative elements and challenges to be faced in the hospital environment. As a graduate, one must consider how they might enjoy the environment of the hospital and a long patient list that needs to be prioritised. The transient nature of hospital physiotherapy can also be a challenge for some physiotherapists, as there is not the same degree of follow-up and continuity of patient care. Once a patient is discharged to the community, they are no longer under the physiotherapist's duty of care; the community physiotherapists, occupational therapists and other members of the multi-disciplinary team will take over. Some physiotherapists can also find hospital work to be distressing or uncomfortable at times. This may be due to seeing people at their most vulnerable and most injured. Advocating for the patient is essential at such times, as is maintaining professional integrity, and keeping actions and words aligned with one's values and the Physiotherapy Board of Australia's Code of Conduct (or professional code within your country of practice).[15][16]

The Private Sector

The private sector encompasses private clinics and companies that employ physiotherapists across a range of areas including disability services, vocational health and work health and safety, neurological rehabilitation, musculoskeletal and sports physiotherapy, paediatrics, and women's, men's and pelvic health.

An Australian study in 2014 highlighted significant growth in the private sector for physiotherapists, chiropractors and osteopaths over the previous 15 years.[17] It cited high growth in the areas of sports physiotherapy and private practice in Australia, the United States and the United Kingdom, and discussed the government push in Australia to reduce reliance on publicly funded positions, meaning these areas are likely to remain strong as career options into the future.

There is a lot of variety in the private sector. Some practices have more of a manual therapy focus, which can take many forms and may include the use of taping, soft tissue massage, trigger point therapy, Mulligan's, McKenzie, Passive Accessory Intervertebral Movements (PAIVMS), high-velocity thrust techniques, and multi-system approaches including craniosacral, visceral and counterstrain techniques. Counterstrain originated as a mechano-adaptive model of treating pain and dysfunction that has been found to reduce pain and palpation tenderness in clients.[18] Learning and understanding a range of techniques can add to a new graduate's 'toolkit', giving them more opportunities to help clients and reduce the physical load.

Some clinics still use electrotherapies such as ultrasound and shortwave diathermy, and the evidence of efficacy is mixed depending on which therapy is being provided. An overall decline in electrotherapy availability and use has been seen over the last 20 years.[19]

Other clinics may have a strong rehabilitation focus with gait labs, Clinical Rehabilitation (formerly known as Clinical Pilates prior to private health insurance reforms in Australia), gyms or rehabilitation areas, and structured classes for strengthening and stretching. The evidence base is supportive of the latter approach – setting people up with home exercises and focusing on rehabilitation rather than manual therapy alone - gets better results, as in the case of non-specific low back pain (NSLBP).[20]

Providing people with rehabilitation programs for home can be incredibly rewarding, and all clinics do this differently, with some offering digital exercise programs and others relying on handwritten programs. Other clinics may not have such a strong focus on rehabilitation and exercise, preferring to focus on manual therapy and refer on for personal training or exercise programs in gyms.

Shifts and type of work hours can vary greatly across the sectors – a 7.25 hour work day might be the norm in the public sector, but in the private sector there can be an expectation of after-hours work or some long days and some shorter days to provide private clientele with options for evening and weekend classes or treatment.

Other things to consider are the time pressures that can vary between settings. In private practice, there may be a long list of patients to see with strictly scheduled appointment times, whereas in the hospital, time pressures may be similar but with more flexible times for seeing patients. Treating new or complex conditions can also be challenging but there are usually opportunities to do some quick research before seeing a client or ask a colleague or senior how they would treat the condition.

It is becoming increasingly popular for physiotherapists to work in a combination of roles. A physiotherapist may work for a few days of the week in private practice and a few days in the community, in aged care, paediatrics, teaching or some other area. This helps to maintain variety, diversify skills and increase employability, and may also give the body a break by adjusting the physical load.

Working with Older Adults

Healthcare requirements in Australia and the world are growing at an astronomical rate. Due to improved healthcare and life expectancy, Australia's population is ageing, and there has been a subsequent growth in chronic disease according to Australian general practice activity data from 2009 to 2010.[21] The proportion of Australians sixty-five years of age and over is currently at 13%, and is set to reach 25% by 2056.

While this is an increasing burden on the health system, it provides significant opportunities for healthcare professionals working with older adults. A thorough understanding of the Aged Care Funding Instrument (ACFI) will be required.

It's such an important service that physiotherapists provide throughout the lifespan – particularly with older adults – by helping people to maintain quality of life and feel supported with their health problems and musculoskeletal injuries. Traditionally, a key focus of physiotherapy has been maintaining functional capacity and mobility. This is still paramount, but the focus has shifted strongly towards community models of care and home rehabilitation, which aim to help people stay at home longer and limit admission to residential care for those needing high-level care at the end of life. This greatly affects the role of the physiotherapist in home rehab – there is much greater scope for helping people to remain independent and at home for as long as possible.[22]

Paediatrics

Paediatric physiotherapists work with children of all ages, from birth to adulthood.[23] Health professionals working in this area need to have knowledge of pertinent issues, as childhood and adolescence bring unique challenges. Paediatric physiotherapy is delivered in a variety of settings, and policy and organisational structures can significantly affect how services are delivered. Some of the clinical areas in paediatrics that physiotherapists may work in include disability (both congenital and acquired), neurodevelopmental and developmental, orthopaedics, cardio-respiratory, oncology and palliative care, musculoskeletal physiotherapy, and child and adolescent mental health. An emerging area for physiotherapy intervention is intellectual disability and Autism Spectrum Disorder (ASD).[24]

As primary healthcare providers, paediatric physiotherapists require an understanding of child-safe environments.[25] Reporting of suspicion that a child or young person may be at risk is a consideration for any professional working with children, and the Australian Board of Physiotherapy provides guidelines under national law to educate physiotherapists on their roles and responsibilities. For the novice commencing practice in this area, the appropriate working with children clearances are required through state or territory government services.[26]

Currently in Australia, there are no documented standard or core competencies for paediatric curriculum in any of the entry-level physiotherapy programs in Australia. As a result, experience in this area among new graduate physiotherapists varies. If paediatrics is an area of clinical interest, seeking volunteering roles, part-time employment or clinical placements in paediatrics can help students and graduates to gain valuable experience and knowledge in this area.[27]

Vocational Rehabilitation, Occupational Physiotherapy and Work Health and Safety

Physiotherapists have the skills and expertise to help patients return to work after incident or injury. With an extensive knowledge of anatomy, kinesiology and ergonomics, physiotherapists in the area of Work Health and Safety (WHS) assess the physical capabilities of the patient, set safe and realistic return-to-work goals, reduce the likelihood of recurrence of injury, and provide health promotion services within workplaces. This may involve workplace assessments to advise on working posture, repetitive tasks, manual handling techniques, office ergonomics, stretching/flexibility exercises and work practices. Any registered physiotherapist can conduct a workplace assessment after consultation with the patient's employer.[28] This area of practice is discussed in more detail in Chapter 10.

Women's, Men's and Pelvic Health

A growing field of physiotherapy is pelvic floor physiotherapy. This area is not typically covered in undergraduate programs in Australia, as highlighted by research from Frawley and colleagues.[29] Pelvic floor dysfunction affects many people in the community and is often under-recognised and poorly managed. There is now a significant body of evidence suggesting that pelvic floor physiotherapy can address this dysfunction; however, physiotherapists don't currently graduate with the knowledge they require to treat these conditions adequately. Postgraduate training is required to ensure physiotherapists possess the skills and understanding of assessment, treatment and the unique medicolegal and ethical issues pertaining to pelvic floor physiotherapy.

Clinical Educator Roles

Becoming a clinical educator is another option for physiotherapists, and at the time of publishing there is no set course or prerequisite training required to become an educator. It is common for physiotherapists to become educators after first working in clinical practice. Benefits of teaching include variety and diversity of work roles, exposure to the university teaching environment and academia, and consolidating knowledge in a clinical area while assisting students to succeed in their undergraduate program.

Academia and Research

The decision to undertake further study is exciting but does require significant research and consideration. It's also a good time to consult with mentors and look at a number of courses across different universities and consider whether part-time or full-time study options are most appropriate. It's wise for the physiotherapist to take some time to understand their 'why' when considering additional study. Is it to become an expert in a clinical area such as musculoskeletal and sports, or with the aim of teaching at university level, or perhaps it's to meet a clinical need?

Health professionals working in direct patient care are in a unique position to carry out research with clinically-driven research questions.[30] Some physiotherapists may wish to take advantage of this and continue working in a clinical role, while others will transition to full-time academia.

A study from South Africa looked at the transition of physiotherapists from clinical practice to academia and found that despite having previous successful clinical careers, participants initially struggled to make the transition and reported initial feelings of uncertainty and inadequacy. The study found that participants actually took between eighteen months and three years to socialise into their new academic role. Informal learning and peer support were highly valued, more so than a formally structured mentoring process. Confidence in developing pedagogy for higher education and contributing to established communities of practice were found to be key indicators for successfully making the shift to academia.[31]

Rural and Remote

Many new graduates and experienced practitioners feel called to work away. It might be in search of a specific or specialised role, a rural or country setting, or for the adventure or life change. For some it's across a border, for others it's across the seas. All roles will come with their challenges and positives, which will depend on the type of role and supervision. Each big career and life choice will shape the physiotherapist, and potentially provide experience that is highly valued and would not necessarily have been gained by staying in one place.

When it comes to rural and remote physiotherapy in Australia, there is a well-documented deficiency of allied health and medical practitioners nationally, and this has a negative impact on communities. Reasons for the poor recruitment rates and retention include potentially reduced professional development opportunities due to being away from metropolitan areas, perceived lack of mentoring and support, and professional isolation. Positives included diverse caseload and relaxed rural community lifestyle.[32]

This type of role certainly has contrasting negatives and positives. Being exposed to a vast array of different clinical presentations – and being the only practitioner there to perform a treatment – can be good for building confidence and resilience. Another benefit is the development of a range of skills that often comes with having to treat many different conditions. The sense of autonomy can be a welcome change compared to other roles that may be much more closely supervised. However, if the new graduate is seeking the support of a bigger team, they may not find this in a rural setting. Every setting will be different, and it is wise to make enquiries before committing to a role.

Starting a Business

This may not be the most popular choice for the novice physiotherapist, but the research suggests that a growing number of physiotherapists do go straight into private practice. Starting up a business independently or in a partnership is an innovative way of gaining experience.[33]

There are many things for the new graduate start-up to consider. Deciding on a business structure (company or sole trader) is first and foremost. Having a well-defined niche may not happen initially but can develop over time. Understanding the strengths of the business and who the ideal clients are will help when it comes to marketing to general practitioners, sports teams or other community groups. It's also worth doing thorough market research to ensure there is a demand for the service.

To ensure a strong vision, a business plan is essential from the very beginning. The astute clinician will also pay for and seek out assistance with finance, accounting and taxation, quality business coaching, mentoring and continual ongoing training and professional development. Beware of overoptimism, warn experts (Wassinger and Baxter 2013, 210), as a failure to plan adequately is common, and coupled with an inflated expectation of revenue or success, this can lead to frustration and stress for new business owners when initial marketing attempts fall short.

"Sometimes you've got to upsell"

Online Wellness Revolution

The online revolution is here and the opportunity exists for physiotherapists to move away from trading time for money in a clinic setting and instead work with individuals or groups of clients online. This might be a one-to-one video call or teleconference, which is a new and emerging trend in the world of physiotherapy. It could also involve provision of online educational materials for physiotherapists or other community groups. For example, a physiotherapist might develop an online course for clients to help them meet their fitness goals.

Why is this method of service delivery becoming increasingly popular? Clients ultimately want long-term sustainable solutions for their health problems, not just a 'quick fix'. When a client attends a physiotherapy appointment and they leave feeling better, their pain might be gone for a few hours or a day or a week. But if they don't change their lifestyle, the problem is unlikely to get completely better. As a wise mentor once said, 'Pain is often just the tip of the iceberg, and there will always be underlying issues that have predisposed the person to injury.' If these issues aren't addressed, the client will continue to come back with pain. Creating a wellness journey for the client, which includes manual therapy, and then delivering part of that journey remotely is one of the newest ways that physiotherapists can empower clients to make changes that improve their lives.

Non-clinical Physiotherapy

It is becoming increasingly common for physiotherapists, speech pathologists, occupational therapists and other allied health professionals to transition out of their clinical roles into non-clinical roles. It *is* possible to create a fulfilling career without having to provide direct patient care. Physiotherapists have a very high level of training relating to anatomy, physiology, pathology and management of disease, all of which are highly valued skills that can be used to create income. Physiotherapists can venture into areas such as health copywriting, education or tutoring, technology, recruiting, health sales and marketing (including sale of medical products and supplies), clinical rehabilitation liaison or telehealth physiotherapy.[34]

When it comes to choosing an area of physiotherapy, there are so many opportunities that it may be overwhelming for the new graduate. It can be difficult to know what to choose and how well an area will suit one's personal and professional life.

Where to Now?

No matter which field the physiotherapist ventures into, they will have to start in the same place as their peers – the beginning. There are no short cuts to experience; it only comes with seeing many clients over time and learning how to manage different conditions. There will always be new prospects and there are many areas to try, so if the first role does not suit, persist until it's time to move on to something new. Keeping a positive attitude and believing in oneself, making the most of contacts and receiving support from mentors are important aspects of any career change.

Questions for Self-enquiry

1. While studying (or after graduation), were you surprised to discover different areas of physiotherapy you weren't aware of? What were they?

2. Which patient groups do you like to work with? What environments do you enjoy best?

3. What does your ideal day look like? Write it out in detail.

4. What type of clients do you see yourself working with in two years' time?

5. What is your five-year plan? Does it involve having a family or travel? Consider the working conditions, hours and type of job that will help you work towards achieving it.

4
Continuing Professional Development and Career Pathways

Anyone who stops learning is old, whether at twenty or eighty. Anyone who keeps learning stays young.

Henry Ford

Professional Development

Professional development is a crucial part of being a physiotherapy practitioner. Around the world there are different expectations for continuing professional development (CPD), and in the US and Australia it is mandatory for registration. In Australia, the Australian Physiotherapy Association (APA) deems that a physiotherapist must accrue a minimum of twenty CPD hours per annum in APA-accredited formal or informal training. Professional bodies rely on self-regulation of CPD, requiring the individual to take personal responsibility for their CPD participation and monitoring to build their CPD portfolio.[35]

CPD is crucial for practitioners for a number of reasons. On a personal level, CPD fills the passion for ongoing learning. Humans in general need to continue to grow and learn to be fulfilled.[36] This comes from Abraham Maslow's hierarchy of needs, which places the five primary human needs in a hierarchy that begins with basic physiological needs, then proceeds through safety and security, love and belonging, and esteem – needs that all must be met before the final need can be achieved, which is self-actualisation.[37] Maslow believed that most mentally healthy individuals follow a path called 'growth motivation', which allows them to reach this peak of the hierarchy through education, training and finding their true potential once they mature.

Failing to continue with education can actually have serious ramifications. Physiotherapists who cease learning may be at significantly greater risk of professional stagnation and burnout due to lack of inspiration. It also reduces effectiveness as a physiotherapist, and may mean poorer results for the client. Without continuing to learn and gather new skills, any therapist may find themselves feeling stuck and lacking motivation.

Professional development provides opportunities for learning new techniques that can be integrated immediately into clinical practice, as well as new frameworks for practice, deepening understanding of a particular condition or area of physiotherapy, and keeping up-to-date with evidence-based practice.

Lecture evenings and weekend courses offer different levels of education, with the former being less intensive and more about practice overview, while the latter provides a rich setting for improving manual therapy techniques. Podcasts, webinars and online courses have also become increasingly popular ways for physiotherapists to consume educational content and keep up-to-date with new research.

Methods for CPD in Australia and around the world have come under scrutiny in recent years. An Australian study by Chipchase, Johnston and Long (2012) reviewed the literature and found that changes in knowledge and behaviours have been reported but patient outcomes have not improved. It is difficult from the small number of studies to ascertain whether the outcomes are due to the teaching methodologies used or the research design. However, on the surface, these courses appear to inform content knowledge but do not correlate with an improvement in patient outcomes.[38]

This study highlighted that if courses are to have a positive impact on patient outcomes, the organisation and delivery of CPD requires review. The responsibility ultimately rests with the practitioner to find appropriate courses and consider the broader context of what they (and by extension, their clients) will gain from each course.

There is no doubt that professional growth and learning requires continued practice and self-reflection. In a busy clinic, time must be put aside to practice techniques, seek feedback, access evidence summaries and reflect on material learned. Practitioners should elect to participate in courses that are evidence-based and feel confident to question the strength of the evidence underpinning material and techniques. Formal courses are not a quick fix, despite what the advertising material may suggest. The path to better patient outcomes requires a long-term approach, with formal course-based learning being one part of the CPD process.

Early on, practitioners might pursue a wide variety of professional development opportunities.

This is recommended for new graduates in order to gain as much experience as possible from a range of clinical areas. Over time, they may hone a niche and focus on specialist areas such as musculoskeletal, women's health or cardiorespiratory.

CPD is an excellent way to develop and diversify skills, and it makes both the novice and experienced practitioner more attractive candidates when applying for jobs. Some employers will help financially with courses, and may subsidise the cost, with the expectation that the employee will consolidate and share their knowledge with the team.

Not all employers will fund CPD, however, and while these courses can be richly rewarding, affordability is an issue. With increasing costs of living, mortgage repayments and bills (on top of student loan repayments), new graduates may find it difficult to pay for courses – particularly the more costly weekend courses. Deciding on a CPD budget and plan at the beginning of each year can be one way for the new graduate to ensure they have the time and funds available. Committing to spending money on CPD in those early years is imperative to continue growth and learning at a vulnerable stage in the career of a physiotherapist, and this need for further education cannot be stressed enough.

Career Pathways: Postgraduate Study, Titling and Specialisation

There is no single linear career pathway in physiotherapy. Some practitioners will develop across two or more areas of practice, or move from one area to another.[39] There are, however, key pathways for taking the undergraduate training to the next level, including honours and master's degrees, a PhD, titling and specialisation. Honours is most often completed as part of the undergraduate degree and provides a small taste of research, with a project and thesis to complete. A postgraduate certificate or master's degree can be undertaken in different clinical areas across several different Australian universities.

When completing a PhD, the focus is on research and the production of original scholarly work. It provides the opportunity for advanced or specialised clinical competencies for professionals who have graduated with another entry-level qualification, such as a bachelor or master's degree.[40]

In Australia, titling is available to physiotherapists with at least two years of practice experience in one of the relevant national groups listed below. The

APA Physiotherapist Title is a measure of career progress and represents a physiotherapist who is highly qualified in a particular area of practice.[41]

The titles awarded by groups are:

- APA Musculoskeletal Physiotherapist
- APA Sports Physiotherapist
- APA Animal Physiotherapist
- APA Gerontological Physiotherapist
- APA Neurological Physiotherapist
- APA Occupational Health Physiotherapist
- APA Cardiorespiratory Physiotherapist
- APA Women's Men's and Pelvic Health Physiotherapist
- APA Paediatric Physiotherapist.

Specialisation is available to titled members who undergo at least two years of additional training in their relevant field of clinical practice. Once a rigorous examination process has been undertaken and specialisation is achieved, a physiotherapist becomes a Fellow of the Australian College of Physiotherapists.

When considering postgraduate study, it is wise to speak with a mentor or contact the university directly and liaise with support staff. Speaking with physiotherapists who have already undertaken training can provide insight into course relevance and how practical it will be to fit the training in around life and work.

Questions for Self-enquiry

1. **Have you got a system or online log for tracking your continuing professional development (CPD)? Keeping your CPD record up-to-date is essential to be sure you are meeting the minimum requirements of your professional association.**

2. What areas of postgraduate study currently interest you? Would you consider doing a graduate certificate, master's degree or PhD and, if so, in what field?

3. Are you familiar with the specialisation pathway and is this something that interests you? Who could you look to as mentors within this field?

4. What are the areas of continuing professional development that interest you the most? Sports, women's health, cardiorespiratory physiotherapy? How can you flag these upcoming courses and make them a priority so that you can shape your career?

5. Have you considered keeping your options open? You will have time to develop a niche as your career unfolds and you are exposed to different areas.

Working with Others

5
The Therapeutic Relationship

The worth of a human being lies in the ability to extend oneself, to go outside oneself, to exist in and for other people.

Milan Kundera

Developing Client Relationships

Physiotherapists are taught to prioritise building rapport. Being able to intuitively connect with someone is an essential part of becoming an exceptional physiotherapist. It takes time and effort to build rapport, and this usually starts with a smile, a warm demeanour and a friendly approach.

One of the common pitfalls, however, is trying too hard to be the client's 'friend.' While a smile and friendly manner are important at the beginning of a session, it is also important to focus on the task at hand. Patients do appreciate when their case is taken seriously, and this is something that can help to build credibility and trust quickly.

Physiotherapists can also fall into the trap of over-communicating. Talking endlessly about the weather (or anything else that comes to mind) can be distracting and inappropriate. While some talking is useful to break the ice, the physiotherapist should keep directing the conversation back to the client and allow them space to answer questions and ask their own. Pausing allows the physiotherapist to listen to the client, apply clinical reasoning to the facts, prioritise goals and formulate an effective treatment plan. Clearly communicating the diagnosis and treatment plan will also help to build trust.

Once the physiotherapist has established a healthy therapeutic relationship, the rewards can be beneficial for both parties.

Like all relationships in life, the therapeutic relationship offers immense opportunity for personal growth. It can also be challenging. While positive encounters are uplifting for the physiotherapist's spirit, negative encounters can be quite difficult and need to be managed with tact, responsibility, accountability and due care. When such situations are handled well, they pave the way for learning and equip the physiotherapist with the tools they will need in the future to prevent or cope with conflict and manage client expectations. The most challenging experiences, while difficult at the time, can reap the greatest growth and reward.

Building relationships takes time, effort and skill. The novice is not only learning about rapport with clients; they are also learning many new skills in the workplace on a daily basis. This intricate balance of learning and applying clinical skills in addition to learning how to relate to people effectively can be a source of stress for the novice. Developing good communication skills is an art, and even something as simple as reading other people's body language and being aware of one's own body language takes time and effort and requires monitoring.

The astute clinician must also be aware of their moods at work. Because physiotherapists work in service provision, a happy disposition is generally expected. This is quite a large expectation – to be happy all the time; particularly because the client base usually consists of people who are injured, unhappy or needing to be consoled, encouraged and reassured in some way. So what happens when this constant expectation to be happy takes its toll?

Compassion Fatigue

One of the three main dimensions investigated by Christina Maslach in her extensive research into burnout (discussed in more detail in Chapter 16) is that of feeling exhausted or drained – the sense that one has nothing left to give.[42] Physiotherapy is a career that demands a considerable amount of listening, followed by an outpouring of kindness, care and physical effort, particularly in more hands-on roles.

Having responsibility for the management of another person's pain can be a large weight to carry. The physiotherapist needs to learn to reduce or remove the expectation that they must single-handedly 'fix' the client. Vicariously experiencing the suffering of another person can be quite disabling, so it is important to learn not to take the client's suffering on board, and instead think and act from a place of compassion. This can be seen in the case of a client who comes in very rudely or abruptly, who may lash out verbally or say something hurtful. These moments can be challenging because the physiotherapist must maintain a calm demeanour and not react angrily. Sometimes the people who behave the worst are actually suffering the most and need our deepest compassion.

A physiotherapist's client load can also determine the way they manage the relationship. One physiotherapist working in musculoskeletal practice may find themselves exhausted by the end of the day after seeing 20 patients, whereas someone in a rehabilitation setting with a smaller list of clients, fewer interactions and a better balance of paperwork or administrative tasks might experience less empathy burnout. Exchanges with patients who are not improving can also be a drain, particularly in chronic or complex pain states where psychosocial issues can further complicate therapy, and lead to the therapeutic process being drawn out and ultimately negative.

Because seeing lots of patients in a day can be overwhelming, learning how to regroup between clients and how to breathe and let it go can be helpful.

Practising self-care and committing to ongoing personal development are essential. This means taking time out, learning to switch off, and distancing oneself from clients' 'stuff'. It's all too easy to take work home. While this can occasionally be useful in cases of healthy reflection or speaking with a mentor, re-evaluation is required if it becomes a chronic pattern.

Practitioners have different ways of dealing with the energy of their clients. Some create rituals that help them to work more effectively in their workspace, such as burning a candle, washing hands, stepping outside for fresh air, or even spraying essential oils.

Not all environments lend themselves to holistic practices, and in a hospital or community centre the physiotherapist may not have creative control over the space. Eating lunch outside or having a coffee and debriefing with a colleague can help process any challenges as they arise. Other strategies relating to burnout and self-care are covered in detail in Chapters 16 and 24.

Some physiotherapists may use religion or spirituality as a comfort, and pray or ask for protection and guidance from their angels, guides, God, or whatever they believe in. This can be a useful way of coping with difficult relationships or challenging moments.

Other physiotherapists may not necessarily need grounding practices, and may find they are able to let go of a therapy session easily. This difference can be due to personality (some people are better at letting things go than others), but it is also a trait that can be cultivated.

Relationships with Families and Carers

If the client is a child under 18 years of age, the therapeutic relationship will extend to the family or carer. Building healthy relationships with others also takes time – to develop rapport, for following up and checking in with phone calls, care plans and clear communication. It's essential that the client and their family are familiar with the practitioner in charge of their case.

The foundation of family-centred practice in Australia is summarised in ten steps:

1. **Treat families with respect**
2. **Work in partnership and collaboration**
3. **Share information completely and in an unbiased manner**
4. **Be sensitive and responsive to family diversity**
5. **Promote family choices and family decision-making**
6. **Base intervention on family-identified needs and desires**
7. **Provide individualised support, therapy and resources**
8. **Use a broad range of formal and informal supports and resources**
9. **Employ competency-enhancing, help-giving styles**
10. **Enhance family strengths and capabilities.**[43]

One study by Tasker and colleagues (2012) looked at mindful dialogues and the therapeutic relationship in home-based styles of healthcare. Carers and families reported that they appreciated a physiotherapist's ability to fit with the family's situation and routine; it assisted them to relax, trust and interact with the physiotherapy process. One family carer described an experienced physiotherapist's ability to adapt to the situation seamlessly: 'She just fits in, that's all I can say – she just fits in'. Qualities deemed to be desirable were: connecting and resonating with their listeners; identified meaning that people ascribed to clinical interactions; and promoted and advocated wellbeing for clients and their carers. It was noted that the physiotherapist had to 'feel their way' through the clinical conversation in order to achieve these aims within the relationships they developed with all members of the family care teams.[44]

These principles can be applied when working with families in areas such as aged care, rehabilitation, musculoskeletal therapy and paediatrics. Challenges can present in any field of physiotherapy, and knowing how to manage and work through each one takes skill and experience. Communicating clearly and consistently will go a long way towards happy clients and families and better therapy outcomes.

Culturally Safe and Sensitive Practice

In Australia, practitioners are bound by the Code of Conduct, which includes an obligation to have knowledge of and respect for the cultural needs and backgrounds of the community. This includes those of Aboriginal or Torres Strait Islander descent, and people from culturally and linguistically diverse backgrounds. As an example, better and safer outcomes may be achieved for some patients if they are consulted and treated by a practitioner of the same sex.

It's also important to acknowledge the social, economic, cultural, historic and behavioural factors influencing health, at both individual and population levels. Examples of culturally safe and sensitive practice might include the provision of translation services when required, and meeting client requests for a male or female practitioner.

Psychosocial Factors

It's important to try to understand clients and their needs as thoroughly as possible. What are their unique challenges? What level of stress are they under and how is that affecting their day-to-day life? A small Adelaide-based study from Mukul and colleagues (2015) found that physiotherapists in musculoskeletal private practice had difficulty identifying a client's psychosocial status, which is a critical element in the therapeutic process. Psychosocial factors were defined as 'intrinsic individual characteristics such as social background, coping styles, education, past and current experiences and the meaning they hold, all of which influence how disability is experienced by the individual'.

These are often described as 'yellow flags' (a concept discussed in more detail in Chapter 13).

The qualitative study involved interviews with physiotherapists with six months of experience or more, and asked them questions to determine the way they identified psychosocial factors in clients. The findings were that physiotherapists generally felt ill-prepared to counsel clients and were unsure which outcome measurement tools to use to effectively assess a client's psychosocial status. Most relied on 'gut feelings' and vague assessment of stress in someone's life.[45]

This study highlights a gap in psychosocial assessment and counselling skills among physiotherapists. Clinicians are best suited to musculoskeletal assessment, diagnosis and treatment, but still need to be able to factor in psychosocial status when developing treatment plans. The physiotherapist must consider whether a particular client with a complex presentation will take longer to get better because of psychosocial issues. They must also determine how best to communicate this to the client and help them to feel understood. Referring on to counsellors or psychologists may be required.

Words Can Harm, Words Can Heal

Remembering that words can both harm and heal is also an integral part of being a good physiotherapist and building rapport with people. Clients come to see their physiotherapist for a service, but they also come for reassurance, kindness and support. The power of positive encouragement and a 'can-do' attitude must not be underestimated. The classic example of the impact that language can have is the physiotherapist telling the client of their 'degenerative spine' or 'bulging disc' – this does not help the patient to improve and may in fact worsen their pain.[46]

Finding the right way to communicate takes practice. Avoid the use of jargon, and tailor the approach to suit the client. It is important to also check in with the client to ensure they have understood what has been explained to them. This is an obligation under informed consent, discussed further in Chapter 13.

Occasionally, a client may speak negatively about another practitioner. Comments about the other practitioner's skill or knowledge (e.g. 'she was hopeless', or 'I felt much worse after that treatment') may be indicators that the client must be handled with particular care. Explaining things thoroughly, ensuring the client leaves feeling satisfied, and a follow-up phone call to check on treatment effectiveness may be required before rapport has been built and trust established. It's essential to not participate in any negative talk about another practitioner, and to certainly never instigate it. Use a diplomatic approach, change the subject respectfully, and consider helpful comments to suggest that things will be different, but without disparaging the other practitioner; for example: 'I'm sorry to hear you've had that bad experience. Let's see if we can try a different approach and turn things around for you.'

All practitioners will at some point make a mistake. Though it may be embarrassing, it's very powerful to own the mistake. When it becomes apparent that a mistake has been made, the best thing to do is not to make excuses, but to identify the mistake and apologise for it where necessary. A small mistake such as forgetting to send a promised doctor's letter or exercise program can usually be redeemed with a sincere apology and by making it right as soon as possible. However, a disclaimer here: keep in mind that if a mistake in clinical judgement, diagnosis or other serious clinical or legal issue has been made, it is wise to notify a senior physiotherapist or employer as soon as possible, before the incident is discussed in too much detail with the client. It may be necessary to seek advice before admitting full liability in some cases.

Being mindful of the words that heal and the words that can harm is vital for good communication and effective physiotherapy. Avoiding language that catastrophises and using affirmative language instead can help the client to think of their diagnosis in a more positive light, with less worry. The physiotherapist must also try to speak in positive ways about themselves as well. The practitioner may say something like, 'I like to be punctual', or 'I like to be thorough'. They may refer to things that are important to them, such as professionalism or keeping up-to-date with research. Clients will remember the words used and may reflect them back to the practitioner at a later stage.

Learning to Listen

While there are some challenges along the therapeutic journey, the rewards can be great if the physiotherapist can be quiet enough to listen and truly hear their client. A positive therapeutic relationship can change a person's life for the better. This is a big part of why physiotherapists do what they do.

Listening and empathising will be easier on some days than it is on others. Being able to sit and listen to someone, without talking over them or finishing their sentences, is extremely valuable and takes practice and skill. Too often the subjective is hurried because of time constraints and the practitioner may not always listen enough. Developing good listening skills helps to reduce the chance of making assumptions about what people need without actually finding out what their needs are. While it is tempting to fill the space by talking, asking questions and really listening to the answers creates the space the client needs to feel safe.

Often, the most important skill to learn is how to validate another person's situation. Phrases such as, 'I'm hearing that this is very hard for you' show that the physiotherapist is listening and reflecting back what they've heard. This skill of reflective listening can be useful in difficult times or conversations, perhaps when a client tells their 'story', cries in the consult, or discusses a very traumatic experience. A simple phrase, such as, 'tell me where I'm wrong, but…' can help to paint a picture of what the physiotherapist thinks is going on, but also provides the opportunity for the client to correct them if necessary. It is important to never underestimate the power of good listening skills, as they can help build rapport and ultimately make or break the therapeutic relationship.

Going the Extra Mile and Patient Advocacy

At the crux of good therapy is the patient-centred approach, in which the patient's wellbeing is primary. Learning to build trust and positive relationships is essential, regardless of the area of physiotherapy. This means following up in a timely fashion, sending that last piece of helpful information, and going that little bit further to make the patient feel respected and cared for. It is the physiotherapist's role to always seek the best outcome for their patients, and may involve advocating for the patient's needs and defending against anything that is going to infringe on their rehabilitation journey (such as workplace issues in a compensable claim).

Building relationships can be hard work at times, and may be more challenging for some physiotherapists than others. Ultimately, it's about human connection. It's about hearing someone's deepest truths, understanding their physical and emotional condition, and knowing how to validate that experience. It's about helping them to rise up again, feel better, move better, and reach their goals. This is what can be achieved when meaningful therapeutic relationships are cultivated.

Questions for Self-enquiry

1. What do you enjoy about working closely with others?

2. What do you dislike or find challenging about working closely with others?

3. How would you rate yourself as a listener? Poor, fair, good, or very good? How can you take steps towards becoming a better listener?

4. Can you think of any examples of times that you have 'gone the extra mile' for a client?

5. Can you think about what appropriate sharing means to you? What parts of your personal life feel appropriate to share? What boundaries do you need in place? Boundaries will be further explored in Chapter 12.

6
Mentoring

Alone we can do so little; together we can do so much.

Hellen Keller

What is Mentoring, and What are the Benefits?

In a Canadian study of physiotherapists (Ezzat and Maly 2012, 84), mentorship was described as any nurturing process in which physiotherapists use their skills and experience to guide, teach, support and counsel a less experienced colleague for the purpose of professional and personal development. Through a series of fourteen interviews, the researchers found that mentoring involved building a shared passion for learning and commitment to the mentee's success. Four key themes were identified:

1. **Building passion**
2. **Keeping fresh**
3. **Making the physiotherapist stronger**
4. **Promoting deeper learning**

Participants in this qualitative study reflected on each of these themes. When it came to 'building passion', one mentee commented on the energy of her mentor and how his enthusiasm for patient care helped to fuel her passion for the profession. Another remarked on the theme of 'keeping fresh' and how a great mentor had encouraged him to keep up-to-date with the latest in evidence-based practice and advance his clinical skills. 'Making the physiotherapist stronger' identified that mentoring makes an individual stronger, but it also makes the profession stronger as a whole. Mentorship was seen as a way of raising the standards of professional practice and increasing the overall reputation of physiotherapy in the community. Lastly, mentoring 'promoted deeper learning' when structured time was set aside for mentee and mentor to work on mentorship goals. Strategies used during these structured sessions included practising transferring academic knowledge to clinical situations, stimulating reflective thinking for better clinical reasoning, and encouraging new and recent graduates to consider the patient's perspectives and the impact that physiotherapy had on their lives.[47]

In additional research, mentoring has been linked with increased job satisfaction in private practice. In this setting, support and mentoring, professional development, team relationships and developing a better understanding of career pathways for new graduates were identified as key areas for development in private practice. The general feedback from respondents of this particular survey was that new graduates felt underprepared to work in private practice. A reform to the physiotherapy undergraduate degree was suggested to improve job readiness, increase private practice clinical experience, and streamline career development pathways and opportunities for mentoring for new graduates to improve their sense of job satisfaction.[48]

The perspectives of the private practice owners were also explored in this research. Practice owners commented that new graduates didn't have a solid understanding of how to work in private practice. This led to steeper learning curves and increased requirements for mentoring. This highlights a greater need for clinical placements in private practice, and suggests that mentoring is essential for both students and new graduates so they are better prepared to work in the field, particularly in private practice. Having a reliable mentor early on can help a new graduate to feel supported, nurtured and more confident as they enter the world of physiotherapy and perhaps be taken more seriously by their clients.

"I owe everything to my professional mentor. People are really taking me seriously now."

As a new graduate, the knowledge gap between what is known now and what needs to be learned is significant, but access to a mentor to ask those difficult clinical questions can be reassuring. Having a mentor allows the new graduate to draw on the knowledge base of someone else who has a vast amount of clinical experience already. This makes the new physiotherapist less dependent on just their own knowledge base. In those challenging moments when a client asks a difficult question, or the physiotherapist is presented with something that's new clinically, it's perfectly acceptable to let the client know that they will speak to their mentor to see if they can shine some light on the issue. It's particularly effective in the case of a new graduate feeling they have already exhausted their own skill set.

Just observing someone with more experience can help the new graduate to learn many things. While complex treatment protocols can be learned in this way, the more subtle tips can also be gleaned in this way – things such as how to gently reassure a patient, when to use humour in the workplace, and the appropriate greetings and light chatter to use with clients.

The need for mentoring and support is highlighted in rural settings, and clinical isolation can have a huge impact on a new graduate. An action-research approach was used in a British study (Stewart & Carpenter 2009, 204) to examine whether an e-mentoring program could effectively support physiotherapists in paediatric practice. The pilot program involved an experienced physiotherapist mentoring two new graduates with no paediatric experience via long distance using a laptop. Education was provided through field notes, questionnaires and videoconferencing. The small pilot study showed that technology and the combination of skilled communication provided an effective tool for clinical support and reduced feelings of isolation. The study presented a good case for consistent mentoring via the internet to assist new graduates to feel better supported.[49]

Finding Mentoring Opportunities

Mentors can be found in all areas of physiotherapy. They may be employers, colleagues or senior staff members. Recent graduate physiotherapists who are highly trained can even become mentors for other new graduates or staff within an organisation.

In a hospital setting, senior staff are trained to advise junior physiotherapists. This may mean that a new graduate has several mentors at different stages, depending on who is available in a given rotation. The benefit of this is that it gives the new graduate broad exposure to different teaching styles, therapeutic techniques and clinical areas. The downside is that there may be a lack of continuity or a deeper, more sustained mentoring relationship.

In private practice, physiotherapists are more likely to receive mentoring from a practice owner, although learning can occur between peers from direct observation or by reading others' case notes and applying different techniques.

While some workplaces offer specific mentorships, this is not always the case. It is worth noting that not all physiotherapists actively enter into a mentee–mentor relationship, despite perhaps desiring one. Mentoring relationships may not be the right fit if one or both parties declines the opportunity or finds communication challenging.

Making the Most of Mentoring

Finding the right fit is crucial so that the benefit is mutual, and both mentee and mentor understand the expectations of the relationship. This can be managed by having a sound agreement at the beginning, either verbal or written, about how the relationship will unfold. As a partnership, mentors and mentees might have a weekly meeting to discuss patient retention, difficult cases or new techniques. Or, perhaps they will arrange to meet when troubleshooting is required urgently. Once both parties agree on what the relationship will look like, it's important to get started by scheduling meetings. Being clear on meeting times, arriving punctually and being prepared for meaningful conversation are essential. Respecting the time and effort that each party takes to be present is important, as is maintaining a sense of gratitude.

Often some of the best mentor–mentee relationships are those that unfold deliberately in the workplace, when an employer has a vested interest in teaching their employees what they know. Employers genuinely wish to see their staff members learn and grow, and strive for the best client outcomes possible.

If a mentoring relationship does not unfold as expected, being clear and honest is crucial. Perhaps there may be a technique or approach that the new graduate actually finds questionable, or does not resonate with. It's important to use clinical reasoning and always question things rather than blindly accepting something just because someone older and wiser recommended it. There may be times when perceived need for mentoring lessens over time as a graduate learns the new ways of a practice and becomes increasingly competent with patient care. The astute mentor will ensure that they do not cease the relationship too soon, or withdraw contact and care without discussing this with the graduate. Ongoing negotiation or 'checking in' may be required to ensure both parties are satisfied.

Mentoring can be a deeply fulfilling endeavour for both the mentor and the mentee, and can add to enjoyment of clinical practice and fostering of healthy relationships. Finding a mentor who can be trusted and with whom one has a good rapport is an essential part of feeling supported as a new graduate physiotherapist.

Questions for Self-enquiry

1. Whether you are a student, new graduate, or experienced clinician, have you ever received mentoring?

2. If yes, why did you seek out a mentor?

3. If yes, where did you find your mentor?

4. If you do not have a mentor currently, can you think of a physiotherapist you could contact to discuss the possibility of a mentoring relationship? Consider former lecturers, heads of departments where you work, your employer or other physiotherapists you know and admire.

5. Would you consider mentoring other physiotherapists or students? How can you take steps towards this?

6. In what way could you show thanks to your mentor? Consider buying them lunch, a cup of coffee, chocolates or sending a handwritten thank you card.

7. Can you consider how you might remain open to learning and being 'teachable', yet still question what you are taught and keep a curious mind?

7
Team Relationships Within the Workplace

The strength of the team is each individual member. The strength of each member is the team.

Phil Jackson

The Employee–Employer Relationship

Working as part of a team provides constant opportunities for growth, both personally and professionally. Physiotherapy teams are varied, with some small and others large, some with several senior staff members or just one principal (or practice owner). No matter what environment the new graduate first enters into, the relationship that develops between employee and employer can greatly impact one's enjoyment of those first crucial years of practice.

Making a positive first impression on a new employer is vital, and this usually occurs during the recruitment and interview process (unless a recruitment agency is involved). It's important for a job seeker to be friendly and adaptable, but also clear about what they are looking for in a job. Transparency is necessary at this stage so that an employer can gauge life stage, drive, ambition and work ethic from the candidate. The candidate also needs this transparency so that they can plan their future and consider how the role will fit into their world.

As an employer, being clear early on about what a typical day might look like can help to ease feelings of disillusionment or surprise in the new graduate during the transition. It's worthwhile finding out the volume of patients, whether there is travel involved, if there is a requirement for running classes, and documentation type and amount (for example, will there be a significant amount of report writing?).

While it is important to put the work in to maintain the quality of workplace relationships, there will undoubtedly be times when relationships become strained for various reasons. This is often not taught at university, and managing this well will depend on how adept the physiotherapist is at navigating different personality types and getting along with others.

For some physiotherapists, the relationship can be challenging from the beginning, particularly if the expectations of the job role are not well outlined. The contract must be thoroughly read through to ensure that elements that were negotiated (such as flexible working conditions, for example) are upheld. This is discussed more in Chapter 14.

Good communication is essential. In the research (Davies et al. 2016), new graduates stated that regular communication with their employer and feeling that their employer was approachable helped with job satisfaction and wellbeing. They also identified that their job satisfaction was reduced when their employer was perceived to be overly focused on making money. (On this note, it's important for new graduates entering private practice to be mindful of the high overheads involved in running a private practice.)

As in all vocations, getting along with an employer takes commitment and effort to build rapport. In some workplaces, this might involve arranging a more formal meeting to discuss any issues that arise, whereas in other workplaces it might be a relatively casual arrangement where the new graduate can knock on the door and speak briefly about clients, workplace structures or other concerns that arise. Being able to speak to an employer openly and honestly is part of feeling happy at work.

When issues do arise, what can be done to minimise conflict and restore harmony?

Conflict Management

Conflict management is often discussed in job interviews, with the candidate being asked if they can provide an example of a conflict in a previous workplace and how they resolved it. It's natural to think of a client scenario, but conflict with a manager or another colleague can also occur.

A range of things can cause conflict within physiotherapy and the employee-employer relationship. Conflict begins when an individual or group feels that others did or will do something that negatively affects their interests, opinions and beliefs, or norms and values.[50]

Perhaps an employer promises safe working conditions to their employees but does not deliver, causing harm or injury in some way. Perhaps the workplace culture was touted as being strong and positive, yet colleagues openly criticise or condemn each other. Maybe there was a promise of work–life balance, and yet the expectation is to work on the weekends, check emails after hours and finish reports at home. Maybe shifts are too long, or shorter than expected. Maybe it's impossible to take leave because there are staffing issues and no one is available to cover shifts.

Whatever the case, how conflict is managed matters. Differences in opinion among employers, employees and colleagues are normal, necessary and sometimes even productive if they are taken seriously and the people involved find a proactive way to approach them.[51] It is wise to seek advice from a trusted work colleague, manager or mentor and work through the conflict quickly and professionally. Seek help from a mediator if required.

When conflict leads to bullying, what can the new graduate do? Looking to the research for guidance, bullying in the workplace has been defined as 'interpersonal hostility of a persistent and frequent nature'. It has been associated with reduced health and wellbeing among those targeted, and has been found to lead to poor organisational outcomes including reduced creativity, increased absenteeism and increased turnover rates.[52] Having policies and procedures for managing bullying is vital. All workplaces need to take responsibility for the health and wellbeing of clients, key stakeholders and employees.

Understanding where communication may have broken down in the first place (and fixing it) is a positive step forward in resolving conflict and bullying. Research has shown that 'symmetrical internal communication' helps to improve both the employee–employer relationship and employee engagement.[53] This method involves establishing trust, credibility, openness and reciprocity, and having a process and time for feedback and negotiation. The research also shows that employees who receive positive communication about their performance tend to be more motivated to maintain trusting relationships with their organisation, which is important for both employees and employers. As a new graduate, being shown appreciation and receiving positive feedback is key to feeling valued in the workplace and can greatly improve employee engagement.

The balance of power in the employee–employer relationship ultimately lies with the employer. It is up to the new graduate to be astute enough to negotiate what they need, to be open and honest in their communication, to understand their learning style and to seek support when they need it. If a relationship has become challenging or difficult, it is essential to resolve it as soon as possible, rather than allowing things to continue unchecked. Speaking up respectfully but assertively can help to clear the air and may even be a catalyst for positive change.

Peer Relationships and Teamwork

Physiotherapy is very much a people and team-oriented profession. As multi-disciplinary approaches to patient care are increasingly the norm, it's the team spirit in hospital departments, private practices and community centres that is one of the most special parts of the physiotherapy experience. There are many positive elements to teamwork – camaraderie, mutual respect, social outings and lunches with colleagues, debriefing in the office and feeling like part of a community.

No matter which clinical path the new graduate forges for themselves, they will undoubtedly be entering a team environment of some kind and working with others. Even if a new or recent graduate were to set up a private practice, it would still require significant liaising with medical practitioners and reception staff at the very minimum. Working with others is a non-negotiable part of the role and is beneficial for avoiding the stagnation that can come from professional isolation.

Peer relationships were identified in a recent study as being a crucial part of job satisfaction among new graduates (Atkinson & McElroy 2016, 57). New graduates and postgraduates reflected that working with others helped them to create a comfortable working environment and assisted in further developing their skills (Atkinson & McElroy 2016, 58), with one graduate in the study stating:

> *I think the better the network of people surrounding you, the more fulfilling it is.*

Team structure and relationships will vary depending on the setting, illustrated by the difference between a rural setting and a hospital environment. In a hospital, there may be times of working autonomously and times of working very closely with physiotherapists or nurses to do 'doubles' on the ward. For the physiotherapist on the road providing outreach in a rural environment, it might involve long stretches of the day working solo, but there is still likely to be communication with other colleagues throughout the day. Working with others might involve joint consults or 'co-treating' with other physiotherapists, or even working online or via videoconferencing to connect with a team or mentors. In most roles, there are times for autonomy and times for collaborating.

When starting out on the career journey and while searching for a job, there are important questions for the new graduate to ask. Does the workplace have a good team ethos? Is communication between practitioners fostered and encouraged? Are there team-building events or weekend invitations (if this is desired)? Are team members approachable and engaged? These are all important factors to take into account when choosing that first role. If it's not clear from the outset, asking questions and speaking to current employees can provide insight.

The Code of Conduct states that physiotherapists must ensure they communicate clearly, effectively and respectfully with other practitioners. This includes behaving professionally and courteously towards colleagues and other practitioners. The Code also states that effective collaboration and communication are fundamental aspects of good practice. This means that all parties within the team need to know their specific responsibilities for patient care. To make sure this happens effectively, the client needs to be informed about the people in the team and their roles. It also means setting a positive example for other team members, preventing bullying and harassment, and supporting and supervising others within the team.

Teamwork is something that needs to be cultivated carefully. It's more than just eating lunch together at the Christmas party; it's about helping and supporting each other every single day and being committed to the team. It's about being genuinely interested in others and making the effort to find out what's going on in their life. It only takes five minutes to ask someone about their day or their hobbies, to express gratitude for a job well done or cheer someone on when they have a win. Having supportive colleagues and a positive team environment can brighten anyone's day and increase feelings of happiness and wellbeing in the workplace.

Questions for Self-enquiry

1. **When it comes to communication with your employer, would you prefer a weekly, fortnightly or monthly check-in? Be clear on your needs and discuss this early to manage expectations.**

2. **What kind of supervision appeals to you? Would you like to sit and observe? Would you like to be observed or co-treat? Would you like support to go over difficult cases? Would you**

like to work somewhere with an 'open door' policy so that you know you can always ask for help when needed? Consider ways to approach your employer and negotiate support when required.

3. How well have you gotten along with previous employers? What made the relationship(s) work or not work? What could you draw on to enrich your new role as a physiotherapist?

4. Random acts of kindness are a thoughtful way to connect with other team members. Consider a small surprise gift, a coffee, or something homemade as a treat for your work colleagues. How could you surprise someone with an act of kindness this week?

5. How could you go the extra mile for people in your team? It could involve making someone else's day easier by photocopying the last exercise sheet, or if co-treating, completing your documentation promptly and thoroughly to make their job easier.

6. Have you ever sought assistance from a third party or mediator to manage a conflict in the workplace?

8
Multi-disciplinary Approaches and Referrals

The richest people in the world look for and build networks; everyone else looks for work.

Robert T. Kiyosaki

Multi-disciplinary Approaches

Regardless of whether a client has an acute or chronic condition, most are reliant on a complex coordination of services involving several health professionals across a variety of settings. When communication is optimum between referrers, clients can expect to feel supported, cared for and understood by their team of health professionals. However, patients and carers may at times describe experiences of 'falling through the cracks' and feeling lost because of poor communication between treatment providers, or lack of continuity of care. To address these undesirable aspects of healthcare, Interprofessional Education (IPE) is being progressively introduced into university-based medicine, nursing and allied health curricula to improve teamwork and to increase the understanding of roles across healthcare. IPE consists of students from different health-related professions learning 'from, with and about each other to improve collaboration and the quality of care'. IPE is delivered through interprofessional learning, which is the actual practice of communication, collaboration and teamwork across disciplines to improve patient care and student learning outcomes.[54]

The findings of a recent systematic review on IPE suggest that patient scenario interventions featuring group work in small teams, as opposed to lecture-based IPE, can lead to improved attitudes towards interprofessional interaction and teamwork and improved understanding of health professional roles.

Reporting and findings regarding duration are limited; however, interventions of less than 2.5 hours were described by participants as too brief. Although it can be concluded from this study that IPE works, understanding of the relationships between different modes of IPE and outcomes is limited and needs further research.[55]

While universities are aiming to bring practitioners up to speed when it comes to working in networks, what is it currently like to be out in the field working alongside other practitioners? How adept is the new graduate at communicating via phone, email or letter to those they need to speak to, including doctors, specialists, case managers and members of the allied health team?

There is the potential for new graduates to feel out of their depth when speaking to other professionals. They may have difficulty articulating treatment plans or communicating patient care; or they may know the research and the techniques but are not able to justify their use. This may occur when speaking with other practitioners, or when speaking with clients. Keeping things simple, being professional and respecting others' time is important. This may mean negotiating to book in a phone call or finding out how much time the practitioner can speak for (they may only have five minutes between clients).

Referrals

General practice activity data indicates an increased rate of general health referrals across Australia during the previous decade, due to increases in referrals both to specialists and to allied health services (Britt et al. 2010, section 5.4).

When being asked for referrals, ethical practice must be considered. Is it appropriate to refer to friends? Is it appropriate to build networks and refer within those networks? Is it appropriate to refer to someone and expect referrals in return?

According to the Physiotherapy Board for Registered Health Practitioners, referral involves one practitioner sending a patient or client to obtain an opinion or treatment from another practitioner. This may involve transferring the responsibility for the care of the patient or client, usually for a defined time and purpose, such as care that is outside the referring practitioner's expertise or scope of practice.

Multi-disciplinary Approaches and Referrals

It's important to exercise good clinical and ethical judgement when referring. It's not appropriate to refer to a friend's practice for the sake of helping that friend. The client's best interests must be put first, and it is important to act with integrity. For example, having a range of trusted therapists in each discipline can be one way to refer appropriately. This affords the client the opportunity to then choose who they think is going to be a better fit for them and they can book accordingly. Other physiotherapists and practices may even choose not to refer to specific practitioners at all, but instead to say, for example, 'you need to see a dietitian' and leave it up to the client to find somebody they resonate with.

While the new graduate doesn't necessarily need to have had firsthand experience with every practitioner they refer to, it can help to meet them and see their establishment. Sometimes it may be appropriate to refer based on reputation or area of specialisation alone. Discretion must be used; communicate clearly with the client and with the practitioner. A professional letter, note or phone call can facilitate a proper introduction and ensure that all parties agree on the aims of the session, which may improve the outcome for the client, and at the very least instill a sense of being cared for appropriately and thoroughly by a team of health professionals.

"I only refer my clients to practitioners who like, watch, follow, link, connect, friend and pin me."

It may be simple for a new physiotherapist to recognise when things are out of their scope medically and refer to a doctor or specialist. What can be challenging are the more subtle referrals – perhaps identifying that someone is struggling emotionally and would benefit from a session with a counsellor or psychologist, or knowing whether to send someone to a podiatrist or naturopath. In these cases, it may be necessary to look to the client for guidance and inquire: 'Do you have a counsellor you have seen before?' Being open while still being gentle and compassionate is a skill worth practising. There is no point in referring a client to another practitioner if they aren't on board and clear about why they are being referred. What will be the benefits of seeing the other practitioner? What will be the risks? Make sure they are fully informed and give their consent before writing a letter or contacting the other professional to maintain client–practitioner confidentiality.

While it's inevitable that physiotherapists sometimes need to refer on, it can be a difficult thing to admit professionally that someone isn't getting better and that their care is now out of the scope of practice. Asking another member of the team to have a look at their case or co-treat is necessary to ensure the best outcome. Sending someone back to their GP for more tests, or referring on to a different modality may be needed when all avenues of treatment within the new graduate's sphere of knowledge and experience have been exhausted. There is almost always something else to try, so the bigger the skill set or better the access to mentors, the better the new graduate will become as a clinician. This will assist the new graduate to better retain their clients as they will be able to offer the client new perspectives and persist long enough to help them get the best outcome without prematurely referring on.

Being able to work within a network is one of the many joys of clinical practice. This process is complex in nature and requires sound clinical reasoning, excellent communication and ethical consideration at every stage. There are many reasons to refer on and every client's unique circumstance needs to be considered. If in doubt, always leave the final decision in the client's hands and check with them before communicating their details to a third party.

Questions for Self-enquiry

1. **What are the key points you need to get across to a practitioner in a referral letter?**

2. Are you a concise communicator or will you need to work on this?

3. Do you prefer the written word, or a conversation with another practitioner? Phone calls can be a great way to communicate if you prefer that style; just be sure to document the outcome of the call in the notes.

4. Have you considered professional ways to refer to specialists and other practitioners so that the best interests of the client and their confidentiality are upheld?

9

Clinical Reasoning, Evidence-based Practice and Outcome Measurement Tools

I believe in evidence. I believe in observation, measurement, and reasoning, confirmed by independent observers. I'll believe anything, no matter how wild and ridiculous, if there is evidence for it. The wilder and more ridiculous something is, however, the firmer and more solid the evidence will have to be.

Isaac Asimov

Clinical Reasoning

The term 'clinical reasoning' describes the process physiotherapists and students use to make informed decisions about patient care and solve problems.[56] It's something that can be intangible and challenging, even though on paper it seems easy enough to grasp. It's a skill that develops over time, and as a wise mentor once said:

After a while you just know what to do, for different conditions, because you have reasoned through so many different cases. The answers tend to come almost automatically, and you find yourself giving the advice and providing the treatment without having to think so hard about every single thing.

That's when a clinician feels their level of experience deepen, and it does make life as a health professional easier. This phenomenon was explored in a review paper of occupational therapists in which clinicians with a high level of professional craft knowledge were found to make rapid and skilled judgements but were unable to articulate how they came upon their decisions.[57]

While there is no research currently looking at the role of intuition in physiotherapy practice, it is known that when treating clients, physiotherapists use four out of five senses: touch, hearing, sight and even smell. These more subtle processes can significantly inform assessment and treatment and may be considered part of the clinical reasoning process.

Research by Holdar, Wallin and Heiwe (2013) analysed ways in which physiotherapists reach clinical decisions.[58] The article found that within the acute setting, physiotherapists often had 'set role codes' and hierarchies, and these external factors also affected their decisions.

This study also revealed that internal factors, such as personality and physical and psychological state, influenced clinical reasoning. One informant described how personal matters could make it more difficult to carry through an intervention or communicate reasoning appropriately during a consult: 'Certain things do not concern your work, but they occupy your mind nonetheless.'

The astute physiotherapist will reflect on both external and internal factors and how they may affect decision-making and problem-solving in the clinical setting.

Evidence-based Practice

Evidence-based Practice (EBP) involves integration of the best research evidence with clinical expertise and client preferences to produce an appropriate and effective service.[59] There is growing pressure on physiotherapists to embrace EBP because it protects physiotherapists to some degree in the event that a treatment is questioned. It enables the practitioner to lean on a body of evidence in conjunction with clinical expertise to inform what they do in physiotherapy sessions. Practitioners can keep up-to-date by reading journals, listening to evidence-based podcasts, and attending in-services, short courses or conferences.

Being discerning about the calibre of studies is important. Tools such as the PEDro scale can be used to assess the internal validity of a research trial and determine whether a study has sufficient statistical information to make the results interpretable.[60] It can also be useful to choose papers that are easily relatable to clients or conditions seen in clinical practice and provide tangible examples with case studies that can be explored. A clear description of the methodology can also help to inform practice, and inclusion of specific exercises or protocols can make results more applicable for the clinician.

One way to stay on top of research is to have a journal club within the physiotherapy department or make it part of regular in-service. At these sessions, team members can present the most up-to-date evidence for a specific topic so that everyone learns at the same time from the research. This keeps practitioners aware of the latest research on different conditions and reminds them how to critically appraise the literature. Setting email alerts for major medical journals can be another way to find out about the latest publications, and it is also important to critically assess the pieces of literature for their applicability.

Educating clients on the latest in research is a great way to empower them. Something as simple as sending a research article to a client (if it will be well received) can build rapport and trust, and help them to stay motivated and confirm they are on the right path.

A prospective observational study with two cohorts (McEvoy et al. 2011) used the Evidence-Based Practice Profile Questionnaire to assess whether new graduates transitioning into the physiotherapy workforce were adequately trained in EBP. The study found that during the first two years in the workforce, there was a transitory decline in the self-reported practice and sense of relevance of EBP, despite increases in confidence and knowledge in other areas. The pattern of progression of EBP skills beyond these early professional working years is unknown.[61] We can hypothesise that in those early years, new graduates are working very hard clinically, attending courses and perhaps not reading as many journal articles as they could be but are learning in other ways.

Outcome Measurement Tools

Outcome measures are crucial as they help us to demonstrate treatment effect.[62] They need to be standardised, have detailed instructions for scoring and interpretation of results, and meet accepted criteria for reliability and validity. While they are an important part of clinical practice in all fields of physiotherapy, certain barriers have been identified that limit their use. These include time, complexity (easier or shorter measures were more commonly utilised), knowledge of their use (which was found to be more extensive among recent graduates and postgraduate students), and culture of the facility.

It's important to use multiple validated tools to assess compensable clients and their injury status. Such outcome measures allow for monitoring the effectiveness of physiotherapy treatment, specifically in relation to the worker's pain levels, physical impairments and ability to perform Activities of Daily Life (ADLs) and work duties. All physiotherapy services should be based on best practice principles to ensure that the treatment provided is appropriate and produces objective benefits. Best practice incorporates physiotherapy treatments for which there is research evidence of efficacy, or for which there is not yet evidence in the literature but there is a basis of scientific theory and clinical expertise.[63][64] Treatment outcomes should be expressed in functional terms as they relate to specific work task capacities. Examples of these are increasing tolerances for standing, walking, lifting, sitting, pushing, pulling and carrying. In addition, treatment outcomes should address improvements in activities of daily living. An estimate of outcomes of physiotherapy care involves comparison of measurements. The first measurement is taken when treatment commences (Baseline Outcome Assessment), and others at later stages. Differences between initial and subsequent measurements demonstrate change that may be attributed to physiotherapy intervention. Other factors such as medications, psychosocial and other interventions must be taken into consideration. When developing a treatment program, physiotherapists should apply their assessment skills and knowledge of clinical reasoning to provide treatment that is reasonably necessary. This will be based on:

- Clearly identified goals of treatment designed to improve functional status

- An understanding of the evidence supporting the efficacy of the treatment

- Estimation of an approximate number of visits and timeframes required to achieve the stated goals

- Measurable, functional outcomes so that treatment can be progressed, and ceased when treatment goals have been achieved

- Consideration given to how the goals of treatment and outcomes relate to return to work.

A study from 2016 aimed to investigate discourses relating to the implementation of standardised outcome measurements within rehabilitation practice. Three focus-group interviews with 25 occupational therapists (OTs) and physical therapists (PTs) in local rehabilitation settings were conducted. Results indicated that although positive attitudes towards outcome measurement were expressed in the professional journals, OTs and PTs in local settings had professional reservations about standardising their assessment. The therapists were caught in what they considered to be a dilemma between taking a holistic approach and performing standardised practice. Systematic outcome measurement challenged the core values of their practice. Therapists often felt that 'it did not make sense' to use outcome measurement or that some of the items were inappropriate for some clients which became a barrier to its implementation. The study concluded that if the use of standardised outcome measurement is to be increased, reflection is needed regarding appropriateness of measures used and how the measurements can be integrated to provide a meaningful contribution to individual rehabilitation processes.[65]

Clinicians have an opportunity to lead the way in Evidence-based Practice. Using research to inform the work ensures that clinicians are up-to-date with the latest changes in treatment techniques, enabling provision of cutting-edge therapy to clients based on evidence.

Questions for Self-enquiry

1. How can you actively stay up-to-date with the research?

2. What databases do you currently use to perform searches for literature?

3. How do you store research papers for your own records, and how do you report your research findings to colleagues and clients?

4. Which outcome measures do you find yourself using most often in clinical practice?

5. Which tools do you use for assessing the level of evidence in each of your studies?

6. Aside from the well-known musculoskeletal measures, have you considered searching online for new measures that you could use for screening depression, anxiety, pelvic floor function or other areas of health and wellbeing such as quality of life?

7. When you first use an outcome measurement tool, how long are you waiting to reassess? Do you have any systems in place to remind you to reassess?

10
Working with Compensable Clients and Third Parties

Learning is not attained by chance; it must be sought for with ardour and diligence.

Abigail Adams

Understanding Legislation, Regulations and Practice Guidelines

In private practice or vocational rehabilitation, a portion of the caseload will be compensable clients. New graduates must take the time to understand the WHS laws relevant to their jurisdiction. Safe Work Australia is the national policy body responsible for the evaluation and development of the WHS laws. Their role is to develop national policy, but they do not regulate WHS laws; each state and territory in Australia has its own Act/s of legislation, which set out the broad legal and policy requirements, and Regulations which specify how the Act should be applied. Peak bodies within those jurisdictions then develop their own guidelines, based on the legislation, to guide clinicians. In South Australia (SA), for example, the *Work Health Safety Act 2012* is supported by the *Work Health and Safety Regulations 2012*.[66] The peak body responsible for governing work health in SA is SafeWork SA; they also oversee public safety and industrial relations.

Work Injuries and Compensation

In Australia, the total cost of work-related injury and disease to the Australian economy has been calculated at $61.8 billion, and in 2019, 64 Australian workers were killed at work. The total amount of workers' compensation paid each year for work-related mental health disorders is estimated to be $480 million. These are sobering yet important statistics, and physiotherapists play a crucial role in helping to reduce risk in the workplace and rehabilitating injured workers.[67]

The astute clinician working in the area of vocational rehabilitation or in private practice with injured workers will refer to their local WHS authority and investigate how the claims process works. It usually commences with initial notification of injury to the employer and insurer. The insurer may make provisional payments to the employee before it determines liability in some cases, and a claim must be made within six months of a worker's injury or accident.[68] A physiotherapist may be involved in supporting a client through this process. It is important to remain impartial and advocate for the client's wellbeing as appropriate, while understanding minimum requirements such as sending reports and management plans only when requested (clinics can charge for time for these and they have their own unique codes), and using standardised measurement tools at the beginning and end of a specified course of treatment.

WorkSafe Victoria has developed the clinical framework for delivery of health services to injured workers.[69] The framework highlights the following principles as essential for case management:

1. **Measurement and demonstration of the effectiveness of treatment**

2. **Adoption of a biopsychosocial approach**

3. **Empowering the injured worker to manage their injury**

4. **Implementing goals aimed to optimise function and increase participation and/or return to work/health**

5. **Base treatments on best available research.**

An editorial piece written by Anne Daly in the *Australian Journal of Physiotherapy* highlights the significant role that physiotherapists play in helping injured people return to work.[70] Her suggested strategies to increase return-to-work rates included the following:

- Ask the patient about their work before they were injured or unable to work, and document the tasks they were doing

- Start a conversation early about work, including setting a date with the injured person about when they expect to be back at work

- Create an expectation that work is part of rehabilitation, not the end result

- Dispel the myth that a person needs to be back to normal or pain-free to work

- Communicate clearly with all stakeholders about the role of physiotherapy, scope and limitations

- Acknowledge and promote expertise in physical health and functioning, and liaise with the workplace and the medical practitioner to facilitate return to pre-injury or modified work duties

- Reflect on words used during the consult and avoid catastrophic language that creates fear and avoidance around activity and work.

Avoid becoming embroiled in system-bashing or clinician criticism, which can fuel anger and distrust toward employers or other health professionals. Clear, respectful communication between parties can make a big difference toward more harmonious exchanges and better outcomes.

WorkCover NSW has appointed a network of independent physiotherapy consultants who provide advice and peer-review of physiotherapy service delivery in the NSW workers' compensation system.[71]

Referral to an independent physiotherapy consultant is intended to achieve the following:

- Consultation with the treating physiotherapist to objectively discuss relevant issues relating to the management of the injured worker, with the aim of achieving the best outcome for the injured worker

- Review of service delivery by qualified physiotherapists with recent clinical experience in the management of work-related injuries, who can provide education and advice about how to achieve good treatment and return-to-work outcomes

- Control of costs by recommending the cessation of service delivery that is not reasonably necessary, or by providing recommendations for appropriate treatment

- Assist insurers and employers to better understand when and how much physiotherapy is reasonably necessary.

In discussions with the insurer, the treating physiotherapist may also request the involvement of an independent physiotherapy consultant. The role of the consultant is to ensure over-servicing does not occur – something the new graduate must be aware of.

Motor Vehicle Accidents and Compensation

Motor Vehicle Crashes (MVCs), also known as Motor Vehicle Accidents (MVAs), are generally associated with diminished mental health, and evidence suggests the process of claiming compensation following an MVC further increases distress and impedes recovery. An Australian study in this area had two main aims:

1. **To investigate whether the client's interaction with the insurance agency was associated with anxiety for the client**

2. **To qualitatively explore aspects of dissatisfaction with the compensation process.**

Results indicated that factors inherent in the compensation process contribute to anxiety. The association between catastrophising and anxiety and depressive mood led the researchers to suggest it is worthwhile investigating further the role of negative cognitions in the compensation process. People who scored highly on catastrophising after the MVC may benefit from early psychological interventions.

Another important stressor is the interaction with the insurance company. Stress is associated with problems in communication, medical treatment, and claim settlement. This study additionally draws attention to some under-recognised problems such as delayed payments.

Proactive Claims Management could address some of the identified issues, which could improve the health of injured people after an MVC.[72] While this study did not specifically look at the role of physiotherapists, they undoubtedly have a large role to play in helping the injured person regain their sense of self. This can potentially take a toll on physiotherapists, and their own self-care is extremely important when navigating compensable client care.

Aims and Challenges when working with Compensable Clients

Physiotherapists are under multiple pressures with this client group, including keeping up with paperwork and administration, not exceeding an appropriate number of treatments, pressure to adequately identify red and yellow flags and address them, and stress from navigating the system. Keeping a positive attitude for the client's sake and avoiding negative talk about workplaces or other practitioners is absolutely essential for professionalism and integrity. For practice managers and clinic owners, working through the extra administration as well as keeping on top of payments from compensable bodies takes time, due diligence and excellent communication with staff and third parties.

It's imperative that physiotherapists respect the guidelines and work with the peak body. Meeting requirements and knowing what they will and will not pay for is essential. Kindness and compassion balanced with a degree of assertiveness and directness can help all parties reach the best outcome possible.

Questions for Self-enquiry

1. What can you do to ensure you understand the frameworks required to work with compensable bodies?
2. How can you support your clients to navigate the system without becoming involved in 'system bashing' or clinician criticism?
3. How can you practice self-care to ensure that your needs are met and that you are debriefing with the right people and feeling supported in your work?
4. Have you read the necessary documentation for your state or region?
5. Are you aware of your requirements as a treating physiotherapist, i.e. use of outcome measurement reporting tools, reporting on treatments and proposed treatment plans?

Challenges on the Path

11
Perfectionism, Over-commitment and the High Achiever

You are imperfect, you are wired for struggle, but you are worthy of love and belonging.

Brené Brown

Perfectionism

Perfectionism is a trait commonly found in health professionals. A relationship has been established between perfectionism, stress and burnout among psychologists and doctors, although this same link has not yet been made for physiotherapists.[73][74]

A review article explored perfectionism among the gifted (Silverman 2007) and defined it in two lights; one positive and one negative.[75] The negative light depicts perfectionism as psychologically unhealthy, which may be counterproductive to the development of people who possess this trait, but does account for some people with perfectionist tendencies. Silverman claims that perfectionists may have underlying issues of low self-esteem, low confidence, procrastination and a propensity to set high standards for themselves, with subsequent experiences of guilt and shame when they don't meet these standards. Silverman goes on to describe the positive traits that allow people who identify as perfectionists to work hard, be willing to try new things (without fear of failure), and learn from their experiences as well as their mistakes. Striving for perfection is essential in the case of elite athletes, scientific breakthroughs and extraordinary works of art, which are all achieved through the perfectionistic personality. These traits have also been linked with reaching higher levels of consciousness, the realisation and fulfilment of one's potentialities (self-actualisation), and a drive to perform great humanitarian deeds.

Silverman reflects on the research of Hendlin (1992)[76] and Greenspon (1999)[77] to provide an alternative viewpoint, which is to consider excellence versus perfection. Excellence is defined as the ability to strive for excellence and derive personal satisfaction from performance. Striving for excellence can indeed reflect healthy self-esteem and involves a strong desire to do well, master a task, challenge oneself and be the best one can be. In contrast, perfectionists are seen as needing to excel purely to bolster self-esteem, which is not considered to be healthy.

It is worthwhile noting that while striving to be better can have positive effects on one's life and the lives of those around them, constantly focusing on being 'better' in the future can cause people to lose sight of the positives in the present. Mindfulness (explored further in Chapter 22) can help anyone to stop and appreciate the here and now.[78] Whether one is striving for perfection or not, it is important to realise that there will be many things on a daily basis that are out of control, and it is beneficial to pause, take a deep breath and surrender. These things include clients who cancel, or don't get better even when it was hoped they would and personal and professional plans that do not turn out as expected.

Perfectionism doesn't just relate to drive – it may be wanting to 'appear' perfect in front of clients, such as by demonstrating an ability to follow protocols in health like eating a balanced diet, following exercise guidelines and keeping fit. While there is little research in this area, it can be hypothesised that the physiotherapist who feels constantly 'on display' may feel a burden to maintain a healthy regime. The practitioner may at times feel scrutinised by peers, family or the community, either for being 'too healthy' or for being seen to be 'unhealthy', such as when ordering takeaway after a busy week, or failing to keep up with a regular exercise regime due to illness, or surrendering to the general demands of work and life. The practitioner may feel internal conflict when giving advice to clients if they themselves are not feeling very healthy. This raises the issue of authenticity and 'practising what you preach'. Clients can see through a well-rehearsed speech about diet and exercise, and they may only take advice seriously if their clinician appears to be healthy, relaxed, and functioning at their best. It's wise to remember that we are all only human after all, and to allow ourselves grace periods when we aren't feeling our usual sense of wellbeing.

It can be daunting for new graduates to work with experienced practitioners and see their expertise and finely tuned skills. For the new physiotherapist with perfectionist tendencies, it can be frustrating to be a novice. One must remember that experience develops over many years and cannot be rushed. Even the experienced physiotherapist who has been practising and mastering their skills for decades has more to learn – the commitment to lifelong learning is something all health professionals must embrace.

Over-commitment

The close cousin to perfectionism is over-commitment. This is defined as 'to commit excessively and therefore obligate oneself beyond the ability of fulfilment'.[79] There are times when the requests of employers and family need to be met, and saying yes to certain demands may be required. At other times it is important to re-evaluate which commitments are taken on and work out what is essential and what is negotiable. Volunteering, committee work, or professional development activities all need to be monitored throughout the year for appropriateness.

One of the best ways to avoid over-committing is to use the twenty-four-hour strategy. When faced with a new request that has no clear answer, taking twenty-four hours to make the decision can be a useful strategy to help reduce over-commitment. This allows time to decide whether the request aligns with one's values and personal agenda. Saying yes when it is not convenient will ultimately lead to resentment and a potentially negative outcome. Learning how to say yes with enthusiasm when you've established that it aligns with your goals and you have time to take it on, and politely and diplomatically declining when it doesn't, is an essential life skill.

The High Achiever

The pathway into physiotherapy may be directly from school or it may be via transfer from another health degree, depending on the educational institution. For the student wanting a career in physiotherapy, human movement, nursing or other health degree (and hoping for a transfer), the stakes are high. Physiotherapy is a competitive field, and it's not an easy course to get into as it typically attracts high achievers with high scores from their schooling. High achieving (also termed a 'proactive personality' in the literature) has been correlated with taking initiative, displaying take-charge behaviour, speaking up and seeking opportunities.[80]

It can be hypothesised that many physiotherapists will be high achievers, so it helps to develop a deeper understanding of how to manage high-achieving tendencies. The notion of the 'good-enough practitioner' was explored by Skovholt and Trotter-Mathison in their book *The Resilient Practitioner*. This theory reassures helpers across many fields that they are indeed adequate, and can and will get by with the knowledge and skills they possess right now.[81]

Being 'good enough' means that no matter where the physiotherapist is on their career journey, they can trust themselves, feel confident in being 'good enough' for clinical practice and commit to mastery at some point in the future.[82]

This 'good-enough practitioner' theory is useful for the novice, as they are particularly susceptible to negative self-talk, which threatens to uncover the novice as a fraud. This concept of feeling like a fraud was termed 'imposter syndrome' by American researchers Pauline Clance and Suzanne Imes in 1978.[83] Imposter syndrome entails holding a secret belief that one is not deserving of success and recognition. This commonly held fear of being 'found out' can be distressing for a new graduate, and even for an experienced practitioner who feels they are not adequate for their role. The good-enough practitioner theory can help the novice to develop sufficient awareness and healthy self-reflection practices to acknowledge their own growth (without expecting to know everything at once).

Also associated with high achieving is the 'Type A' personality. The Type A personality, originally described by Friedman and Rosenman (both cardiologists) to assess the behaviour of cardiac patients, has now been renamed as the Type A behaviour pattern.[84] This behaviour pattern is characterised by competitiveness and striving. It is broken down into two separate components: (1) Achievement Striving, which is characterised by hard-driving task orientation, taking one's work seriously and expending effort to achieve; and (2) Impatience/Irritability, which reflects time urgency, anger, hostility, and aggressiveness (this may be overtly expressed or internalised). Research shows that Achievement Striving is positively correlated with academic and occupational success, whereas Impatience/Irritability is correlated with poorer health outcomes including increased risk of coronary artery disease.

Other literature on this subject from Ryckman et al. (1990) proposes the notions of personal development competitiveness versus hyper competitiveness.[85] People displaying traits of personal development competitiveness have learned to compete *with* rather than against others to achieve their personal goals. They may focus less on the task outcome and more on the enjoyment inherent in the task itself, which leads to task mastery, self-discovery and self-improvement. In comparison, hyper competitiveness is similar to the Impatience/Irritability subtype, with traits of hostile aggressiveness and the need to win at all costs. Low self-esteem, reduced interpersonal trust, dogmatism and the need to control others may also be elements of this personality trait. Understanding these subtypes among employers and colleagues may help to reduce conflict in the workplace and enable practitioners to work to their strengths.[86]

Setting exceptionally high standards, pushing too hard to achieve and failing to schedule breaks for relaxation can be troublesome attributes of the high achiever. But on the positive side, these attributes (when kept in check) can help a novice to better meet the needs of their clients and ultimately fulfill their own potential.

Questions and Exercises for Self-enquiry

1. Have you ever found yourself overly focused on competing against yourself, or with colleagues, peers or loved ones? What strategies can you use to concentrate instead on healthy competition that focuses on competing with rather than against? Would you consider seeking counselling or support with these behavioural tendencies?

2. Do you have any tools or strategies to still your mind when you are having worrying thoughts or noticing perfectionist tendencies? Try using affirmations to still the mind, such as 'I am good enough. All is well, everything is working out for my highest good and my clients' highest good.'

3. Do you ever feel worried that you don't know the answers to a clinical problem? In times of uncertainty or if things are outside of your scope, remember that it's okay to not know it all. Do your research in a timely manner, and seek guidance from a mentor or more experienced practitioner if further clinical support is needed.

12
Professionalism, Social Media and Confidentiality

Wise men speak because they have something to say; fools because they have to say something.

Plato

Professional Boundaries

How much to share (or not to share) in our modern world, has become a very hot topic. How should physiotherapists portray themselves in person, in the clinic and on social media?

Physiotherapists are generally people-oriented, easy-going, friendly and kind-natured. The challenge for physiotherapists is maintaining boundaries with clients, sharing appropriately and knowing what information needs to be kept private (both their own personal information and that of the client).

Boundary setting can be viewed on a spectrum, with solid foundational boundaries at one end (for example, clear start and finish times, minimal or no emailing after hours, no work is taken home, going for a walk at lunchtime), and at the other end, the opposite (frequently working overtime, working through lunch, taking work home). It can be hypothesised that the latter method leads to overwork and burnout if left unchecked.

Inappropriate Care

There are guidelines that clearly define what constitutes appropriate and inappropriate care. According to the Code of Conduct, good care includes the following:

1. **Never using a professional position to establish or pursue a sexual, exploitative or otherwise inappropriate relationship with anybody under a practitioner's care; this includes those close to the patient or client, such as their carer, guardian, spouse or the parent of a child patient or client**

2. **Recognising that sexual and other personal relationships with people who have previously been a practitioner's patients or clients are usually inappropriate, depending on the extent of the professional relationship and the vulnerability of a previous patient or client**

3. **For the physiotherapist who is used to laying hands on a client, there may be a potential risk of the evolution of sexual feelings. This is a highly contentious topic, as sexual relationships are clearly against the Code of Conduct.**

This topic was explored in more detail in an observational study in Australia by Cooper and Jenkins (2008) who looked at the sexual boundaries between physiotherapist and client and whether they differed between male and female physiotherapists.[87] Respondents were asked to state: (1) their perception of the behaviour of a hypothetical physiotherapist in six vignettes highlighting professional sexual boundaries; (2) the incidence of sexual attraction between themselves and their patients; and (3) the course of action they would take in a situation of alleged sexual misconduct between a physiotherapist colleague and a patient.

Respondents thought the physiotherapist's behaviour to be wrong in four of the six vignettes; 65% of respondents thought it acceptable for a physiotherapist who provides physiotherapy services to a rugby team to go on a date with a team member; 74% of males and 41% of females reported having felt sexually attracted to a patient; respondents were aware of a colleague who had dated a patient (33%) or ex-patient (60%). When presented with a vignette describing alleged sexual misconduct, 83% of respondents stated they would advise the patient to make a written complaint to the appropriate disciplinary body. Those who stated that they would personally report their colleague to the Physiotherapists' Registration Board accounted for 19% of respondents; and 15% said they would report their colleague to the Australian Physiotherapy Association National Professional Standards Panel. The variation in responses to the vignettes, the reported incidence of sexual attraction and dating of patients, and apparent confusion about the complaints process identifies the need for improved education in Australia.

Social Boundaries

Students are often warned about the risks of treating friends and family. This is a contentious issue – physiotherapists are naturally drawn to helping others and enjoy helping friends and family; however, the consult can often be incomplete. Family members may not disclose all of their health details during the informal 'consult' as they would with a physiotherapist they did not know, and follow-up and continuity of care might be lacking without a formal structure, particularly if treatment is performed at home or in a social setting. It is crucial that a new graduate encourages relatives to seek other practitioners' help when the graduate's limitations have been reached. It is wise to be cautious and ready to refer people on when their treatment is out of scope.

The Code of Conduct contains guidelines around professional boundaries for the provision of services to family, friends, work colleagues or others in close relationships. The Code highlights that this kind of service can be inappropriate due to lack of objectivity, possible discontinuity of care and risks to the patient and practitioner. If a practitioner does choose to provide care for their family or friends, it's important that adequate records are maintained, confidentiality is upheld, adequate assessment occurs, appropriate consent is obtained, judgement is not impaired by the relationship, and both parties remain open to discontinuing care if necessary.

Professional and social boundaries are essential for safe and effective clinical practice. They are healthy and necessary and need to be applied in all sorts of life situations, not just in clinical practice. For the new graduate, setting boundaries early on can help them to feel in control of clinical care and their employment. Boundaries can also be considered as part of self-care.

Social Media and Marketing

With increasing use of social media, the professional lines can blur. Social media platforms are used by physiotherapists to interact, communicate and promote their products and services. A literature review assessed social media use in healthcare – physiotherapy in particular – and five key themes were identified: privacy/confidentiality breaches; student use and the need for guidance; the patient–therapist relationship and boundary blurring; integrity and reputation of the profession; and a lack of institutional guidelines.[88]

This study looked at the advantages and disadvantages of social media in the healthcare professions, building on research already performed by the Australian Medical Association. With regard to benefits, social media can be an opportunity for practitioners to provide relevant, up-to-date information for the patient and other healthcare professionals. Social networking can enhance camaraderie between colleagues, provide physiotherapists with the opportunity to have a professional presence online, and present an opportunity to widely disseminate public health messages. Further to this, use of social media can improve public relations and help to boost public profile and identity.

The disadvantages, however, can include errors in judgement. It's essential that practitioners meet the same professional standards and obligations online as they would face-to-face. Practitioners must be aware of the implications of their actions online and of their ethical responsibilities, including patient confidentiality and advertising guidelines according to the Health Practitioner Regulation National Law. Breaches of these guidelines can lead to penalties.[89] Physiotherapists are required to seek out these guidelines through the Code of Conduct within Australia, or the relevant institution within their country of practice.

Physiotherapists might often find that clients want to take the relationship further and socialise outside of work or become friends through social media. This is generally not recommended. Of course, it can be more challenging when clients are real-world friends before they become clients. Therefore, it's important to maintain professionalism and practice within the Code of Conduct, no matter who the client is.

Some physiotherapists may never have issues with social media or boundaries, while others may experience significant difficulty. Every case is going to be different, so the novice will need to make decisions about their own social media policy and review those regularly.

Texting

Text-messaging clients is something that physiotherapists often do from a clinic computer or from their own personal phone (particularly in small business); it may also be done by reception staff on the physiotherapist's behalf. It's a convenient way to communicate with clients quickly and easily and may be more readily responded to than email.

But texting can lead to exchange of sensitive information, and research looking at the use of texting between doctors and physiotherapists and their patients indicated that while texting is commonly used to communicate test results and other information, it is a privacy concern.[90] In the field of midwifery, texting between a midwife and a pregnant mother ultimately led to the death of a baby, as reported by Basevi, Reid and Godbold (2014). During the inquest into the death, the coroner reported text messaging to be an 'inappropriate' way for a midwife to conduct an assessment. Interestingly, the father of the baby commented on the use of texting, saying, 'We didn't think it was inadequate at the time – it's the world we live in'. This study concluded that further research and qualitative interviews are required to help shape clinical guidelines in this area.

Confidentiality

Confidentiality is a complex issue, especially in the digital age. It is essential to be vigilant when seeking permission from a client to disclose information to a third party. It's not appropriate to debrief about clients on the bus or at the pub or in other public places, and physiotherapists must not discuss any aspect of a client's treatment – to do so would be a breach of confidentiality.

Many physiotherapists don't realise the extent of confidentiality, and they can end up in trouble as a result. For example, a husband and wife who both attend a physiotherapy clinic for treatment on different days of the week should still be covered by confidentiality; a physiotherapist can never assume how much information people share with their spouse.

It is not up to the physiotherapist to decide what information is public. For example, a physiotherapist might be out with a group of friends and run into a client they have been treating. The client wishes to talk publicly about their physiotherapy. While it's acceptable for the *client* to bring up their therapy, it would be inappropriate for the physiotherapist to divulge that information.

According to the Code of Conduct, practitioners have ethical and legal obligations to protect the privacy of people requiring and receiving care. This means that practitioners and staff will hold information about them in confidence unless release of information is required by law.

This also requires practitioners to treat information about patients or clients as confidential and to apply appropriate security to electronic and hard copy information. Practitioners must seek consent (and in some situations have the client sign a release form) before disclosing information to third parties or another clinic. They must also keep up-to-date with legislative requirements in their state or territory; make sure that the clinic or therapy surroundings are safe and private; ensure that staff are aware of confidentiality while speaking in public areas such as reception desks or nurses' stations; and maintain confidentiality during all social media and online exchanges.

Confidentiality is an extremely important and sometimes overlooked aspect of patient care. It must remain an integral part of care at all times. It is important to be mindful of the right of others to privacy, and when unsure, always err on the side of caution.

Questions for Self-enquiry

1. How do you set limits or boundaries with social media and texting?
2. How well do you uphold client confidentiality?
3. Can you think of any situations where you have unknowingly breached confidentiality?

13
Informed Consent, Documentation and Medico-legal Matters

To be sure I must; and therefore I may assume that your silence gives consent.

Plato

Informed consent means that the client has agreed, verbally and/or in writing, to a treatment, with full understanding of what that treatment involves, the risks associated with the treatment and the expected outcomes. It means that the practitioner has appropriately explained what will occur during a treatment session. It is important to remember to continue to seek consent throughout a session and treatment (not just at the start), particularly if using a range of techniques or treatment methods. This also means that at the beginning of each new session, a treatment protocol needs to be renegotiated. A practitioner cannot assume that the same treatment, performed previously, is acceptable again today; new consent must be sought each time.

Informed Consent

Informed consent is an essential part of communicating with a client and ensuring that a physiotherapist is protected against litigation. It is defined in the Code of Conduct as 'a person's voluntary decision about healthcare that is made with knowledge and understanding of the benefits and risks involved'. Good practice involves providing information to patients or clients in a way that they can understand, then obtaining their verbal and written consent before undertaking examination or providing treatment at every episode of care. It's also wise when referring on for investigation or other treatment to explain clearly what the client can expect, and advising them of any additional or hidden costs which they may wish to clarify before proceeding. When working with clients with diminished capacity for consent, the consent of the patient or caregiver must be sought in writing.

Other treatments such as dry needling may also require separate written consent.

A study by Delany (2007) found that physiotherapists defined informed consent as an implied, rather than an explicit part of the consult.[91] Assuming consent and failing to seek explicit verbal and written consent during both assessment and treatment is a breach of the Code of Conduct.

An Australian study by Magarey et al. (2004) looked at the process of informed consent used by physiotherapists undertaking high velocity techniques (HVT) of the cervical spine.[92] Specifically, pre-manipulative testing was under scrutiny in a bid to assess compliance with the Australian Physiotherapy Association's guidelines (which have been updated since this study was first published).[93] The study found that the use and interpretation of informed consent among members of the musculoskeletal physiotherapy group were variable and that the risk of adverse reactions from manipulative physiotherapy practice, including cervical manipulation, appeared to be very low.

The Magarey study also described negligence for physiotherapists. Under the tort of negligence, if a breach of duty of care can be proved, with the direct result being that the patient undergoes some foreseeable harm, negligence on the part of the physiotherapist is said to have occurred (Brazier, 1992). A duty of care covers the provision of information and obtaining consent as well as the treatment itself. Therefore, providing information and gaining consent for cervical manipulation protects the physiotherapist from legal action, in addition to respecting the patient's right to self-determination.[94]

When situations do arise that cause angst, it is important to remain calm and act in an ethical manner and document appropriately. Being proactive immediately to find a resolution is important. Seek help from a mentor or senior physiotherapist in such cases.

Children and Young People

When it comes to caring for children and young people, it's important to place the interests and wellbeing of the young patient first and consider their capacity to make decisions and understand instructions. Practitioners need to communicate clearly at an age-appropriate level, reduce the use of jargon and ensure that information is provided in a form that the child can understand. Being able to communicate effectively with minors is essential to patient and family satisfaction and practitioner integrity. The AMA guidelines also require that when treating or assessing a minor, a parent or guardian must be in the room, and written consent from the adult and verbal consent from the minor must be obtained before assessment or treatment is commenced.[95]

Practitioners must also have the appropriate Working With Children Checks (as discussed in Chapter 3) and have a responsibility to be aware of their reporting requirements and the circumstances in which they must notify appropriate authorities.

Documentation

Clinicians must learn to tolerate and even embrace the ever-present written work that comes with the role. All healthcare practitioners have a duty of care to the client and are expected to keep appropriate documentation of all interactions, including face-to-face consultations, emails and phone calls. Paper notes are quickly becoming obsolete as software is more readily available as a means of notetaking. The traditional 'SOAP' format for notetaking involves recording of Subjective, Objective, Assessment and Plan, and has been modified with the addition of treatment (Rx). This format remains a consistent part of the physiotherapy undergraduate degree and master's programs across Australia.[96]

Documentation has multiple purposes. It is a means for communicating the treatment provided to a client; it can aid another physiotherapist taking over the case; it creates a living document of a client's medical history; it is used to communicate to third parties, including doctors; and it is essential in case of a civil claim of negligence.

A study from Nigeria by Olawale, Akodu and Tabeson (2015) conducted analyses of physiotherapy records in a hospital, with a total of 503 paper case files from the four units of the physiotherapy department being examined for accuracy. The study aimed to quantify the accuracy of record structure, admission data, physiotherapy examination, physiotherapy diagnosis, patients' prognoses based on the plan of care, physiotherapy intervention, progress and outcome evaluation, legibility, and discharge plan. Results indicated that documentation made in the hospital for the period of this study did not conform to the guidelines of the World Confederation for Physical Therapy (WCPT). The researchers deemed that the accuracy of physiotherapy documentation in Nigerian hospitals needs to be improved in order to promote optimal continuity of care, improve efficiency and quality of care, and recognise patients' needs. It was hypothesised that implementation and use of electronically produced documentation with templates for each section might help physiotherapists to organise their notes more accurately.[97] Further research is required in this area to capture the current status of Australian documentation.[98]

The Australian Code of Conduct requirements for maintaining health records include keeping accurate, up-to-date, factual, objective and legible records that report relevant details of clinical history, clinical findings, investigations, information given to patients or clients, medication and other management in a form that can be understood by other health practitioners. It must be ensured that records are held securely; are not subject to unauthorised access, regardless of whether they are held electronically or in hard copy; are respectful to patients or clients and do not include demeaning or derogatory remarks; are sufficient to facilitate continuity of care; and are completed at the time of events or as soon as reasonably possible afterwards. The rights of patients to access information contained in their health records and the prompt transfer of health information when requested by patients or clients must be recognised.

There are different pressures in different environments when it comes to documentation. For the physiotherapist in private practice, getting all the notes, exercise programs, urgent doctor letters and other documentation up-to-date before going home at the end of a shift can be time-consuming and stressful. In a hospital setting it can be just as difficult, with different pressures. No matter the environment, there will always be paperwork to do, and it is part of the work. Learning to be thorough at all times protects the patient, the practitioner and the team – if one team member is absent, someone else will be able to continue patient care.

George was known for his focus and attention to detail

Changes to Documentation and E-health Records

What is currently occurring, and will continue to occur over the next few decades, is the rapid emergence of new technologies and e-health records. Australia implemented the My Health Record in 2012, which is an online summary of patients' key health information including prescriptions, allergies, investigations and diagnoses.[99] Healthcare providers such as doctors, specialists and hospital staff can access an individual's My Health Record when they need to, including in the case of an accident or emergency. This system aims to improve health outcomes and care by increasing consumers' and care providers' access to health information, improving consumers' knowledge about their own health conditions and providing a way to track health status over time. However, usability issues have been identified particularly among people with low e-health literacy.[100]

There are other popular online programs gaining momentum, including apps to record and track exercise progress that enable videoconferencing to be set up with clients. These bring some advantages such as improved access to healthcare information and improved compliance with therapy.

Medico-legal Matters

Physiotherapists are in a position of power and authority, yet must also manage the inherent risk that comes with that responsibility. Following a typical risk management model, risk identification and assessment are important first steps. Once risk has been identified and assessed, it is possible to problem-solve, implement changes and evaluate how effective the changes have been.

Every practitioner has a duty to exercise reasonable care, skill and judgement when examining, diagnosing, treating and advising patients. Medical negligence occurs when there is a breach of that duty of care and a practitioner can be found liable for any harm caused.

Due to this potential risk, physiotherapists must be adequately registered and have sufficient professional indemnity insurance in the event of legal action. Legal ramifications may include civil litigation (being sued) and deregistration for misconduct. Checking that a policy provides adequate cover is wise, and physiotherapists in Australia need to have a minimum of AUD $5,000,000 and can have up to $20,000,000. Understanding things like run-off cover is important (which is how long a physiotherapist will be covered if they stop paying their premium; for some companies it is lifetime, while for others it may only be a set number of years). Be sure to read the fine print and ask the right questions before commencing a policy.

There are also other instances in which a physiotherapist may be called on by the law, such as validating a course of treatment or giving evidence in court as part of a compensable case.

It's important to remember that claims can be made against even the most careful practitioners. The best thing a clinician can do is to make themselves available to the client and deal with complaints promptly. Calling to check in with a client a day or two after therapy may be appropriate in some settings, particularly if there was an adverse event.

Any red flags and yellow flags must be addressed and documented carefully during treatment. Red flags can include (but are not limited to) serious issues such as bladder or bowel dysfunction, history of cancer, night pain, saddle anesthesia or upper and lower extremity neurological deficits. Yellow flags are less serious and cover features such as thoughts, feelings and behaviours that can impede treatment effectiveness. These might include unhelpful beliefs about pain, or expectations of poor treatment outcome or delayed return to work.[101]

Always refer on to a medical practitioner for urgent further assessment if in doubt. It pays to remember that the main role of a physiotherapist is advocacy for the patient, and if a bony injury or other injury that requires immediate medical attention is suspected, it must be made an urgent priority.

Being proactive to build healthy relationships and prevent relationship breakdown is key for physiotherapists. This begins with identifying the patient's needs and being clear about one's intentions. Never assume anything. Assumptions regarding a client's progress, symptoms, or their wishes for treatment can lead to miscommunication. It's better to over-explain and provide plenty of room for questions than to find out that the client is unsure about their diagnosis or treatment but has felt unable to express that.

When a complaint is made or a formal notification is received by the Board, good practice includes acknowledging the patient's right to complain; working with the patient to resolve the issue where possible; providing a prompt, open and constructive response, including explanation and apology if appropriate; and ensuring the complaint doesn't adversely affect the patient's care (in most cases, referring to another practitioner will be indicated).

Clinicians have a duty of care to ensure that they diagnose to the best of their ability. Treating someone without adequately diagnosing may be considered malpractice. If this means sending clients for diagnostic imaging or working with general practitioners or specialists to ensure a clear diagnosis, then this is the best course of action before treatment progresses too far.

One final legal area of clinical practice that is important to raise is that of defamation. Defamation is where one person publishes a statement about another that is not true and causes people to think differently about that person, often negatively. It covers damaging the reputation of a person or brand, and this includes on social media. One of the first cases of social media defamation was when a student tweeted defamatory remarks about a teacher and was ordered to pay compensation to the teacher. It is important to be very careful when posting about other people, products or businesses.

Medico-legal matters are serious and can be life-altering for physiotherapists. Practitioners must know the rules to protect themselves and their patients, and should seek professional support and mentoring if unsure about the risks and how to manage them.

Questions for Self-enquiry

1. What are some ways to minimise the risk of a complaint being made against you?

2. What would you do if you made a mistake or committed an act of negligence (failure to take due care) during a treatment session?

14
Remuneration, Contracts and Leave Entitlements

A wise man should have money in his head, but not in his heart.

Jonathan Swift

Adequate Remuneration

How do physiotherapists put a price on the work that they do? Physiotherapists lay hands on, advise, guide, support, encourage and so much more. And yet it is not just a calling, it is a vocation that involves the exchange of service for a fee.

Data from Australia suggests the average salary for a physiotherapist in 2019 is $44.77 per hour. Salary estimates are based on 3,031 salaries submitted anonymously by employees, and collected from past and present job advertisements.[102] Data from another source put the median physiotherapy wage in Australia at $65,230 per annum.[103]

Being rewarded for one's professional work is vital, particularly when a significant financial investment in study has been made, whether that is upfront or via a student loan. It is important for a physiotherapist to feel adequately remunerated in order to pay back their debt, but Australian research suggests otherwise, with results from a survey of 561 South Australian physiotherapists indicating that participants believed their remuneration was too low. This same study reported that 75% of physiotherapists chose their profession in order to be financially secure.[104]

Understanding the Award

It pays to be discerning when considering a role. Whether the role is contract-based (hospital), permanent or casual, it's empowering for a physiotherapist to consider that they do have a voice and can negotiate a fair pay structure for themselves. Knowing entitlements and checking the award (without relying on the employer to do the right thing) is essential. So just how much should physiotherapists be getting paid?

Physiotherapists employed in private practice in Australia are covered by the Health Professionals and Support Services Award 2010 (with the exception of those who work in unincorporated practices in Western Australia).[105] Each staff member will have a classification that is dependent on their duties, experience and qualifications.

Because an employer is almost always in a position of power, it's wise to ask the difficult questions during an interview, such as whether a retainer or base salary will be paid in private practice, what percentage of consult fees will be paid, or whether leave is part of the provisions (legally it must be, except in the case of casual employment). In Australia, the Fair Work Ombudsman can investigate or advise on remuneration, and it pays to look up the Award and check which level of pay is appropriate for the individual based on experience.

Understanding hours of work and penalty rates is also necessary. An employee can work up to a maximum of ten hours per day. For every four hours of work, an employee is entitled to a ten-minute paid tea break, and after working for five consecutive hours an unpaid meal break of thirty minutes is a requirement by law. Check the penalty rates for the award to be sure that you are being paid appropriately for overtime and loading for Saturdays, Sundays and public holidays.

There may at times be a temptation to be dissatisfied with wages no matter which clinical area the physiotherapist works. There might be additional administrative demands on top of time spent with a client, which can lead to feeling overwhelmed and potentially disgruntled. Doctor's letters, notes, emails and exercise programs all take time to complete, and particularly in private practice there is a temptation to think these tasks are unpaid. However, reframing this is important, as the client has paid for this full service and everything it entails. There are often high overheads in a private clinic – power bills, reception staff wages and many incidentals that the novice might not think of, such as laundry costs.

Asking for a pay rise is not something that is often discussed at university. The best time to ask is after a successful project launches, or when job performance has been high. If the individual's performance has been low, or they have taken a number of sick days recently, it may not be a good time to ask. Timing is everything. Inflation is roughly 1% per annum, so the new graduate would be wise to ask for a pay rise that at least matches this annually – everyone has to meet the cost of living. Employers will generally be more willing to give a pay rise provided an employee can demonstrate that they add value to the team. This is particularly the case in private practice and would mean that the physiotherapist is doing some of their own marketing and bringing in business for the clinic, not just treating the clients that have been provided for them.

Casual employment is another form of employment that is sometimes offered to new graduates. A casual employee won't receive leave entitlements, but will be rewarded with 25% loading and greater flexibility. A casual conversion clause was added to the Award in 2018 to allow regular casuals to request permanent employee status after 12 months. When negotiating, the new graduate must be sure of what their priorities are.

It is wise to review a new contract with an external support person such as an accountant or mentor prior to signing. While the employer would ideally be given the benefit of the doubt, it is good to check that superannuation payments, long service leave and increases in the award are applied.

Employee, Subcontractor or Self-employed

For those not in permanent full-time employment, leave can be challenging. Subcontractors and casuals receive no maternity, paternity, personal or holiday leave provisions. While this may be reflected in a higher hourly rate, other costs must be considered such as state of the art equipment (if working from home), or increased insurance costs (e.g. income protection insurance).

New graduates must develop a clear understanding of what it means to be an employee (full-time, part-time or casual) versus a contractor. It can be a difficult industry to navigate, so education is vital. An employee has an hourly rate, has tax paid for them, is entitled to superannuation and has an arrangement regarding leave entitlements. They may also be offered a bonus on top of their hourly rate if they hit particular targets. In contrast, a contractor must have their own ABN, gets paid either a percentage of takings or charges for their time at a particular rate, is paid in a lump sum and must pay their own tax. They have no superannuation entitlement or paid leave, but can take as much or as little unpaid leave as they like. Checking these entitlements prior to signing a contract is a wise thing to do.

For the self-employed, it's important to do plenty of preparation, planning and calculations before starting a business (covered in more detail in Chapter 3). The benefits of being self-employed include being able to take holidays without having to request them, and having the flexibility to be available for family events or children's sports days.

Holiday Leave

In the Australian workforce, it is standard to have four weeks of annual leave a year. People often save their holidays until the end of the year and take them over summer in one long continuous break, or in blocks over school holidays if they have children. Regardless, human beings are not designed to work consistently for months on end without a pause.

Failing to take regular leave is a common pattern that new graduate physiotherapists are particularly vulnerable to, though even experienced practitioners can fall into this trap. Forgetting to book leave, or booking leave too far in advance and in one big portion may lead to stress and burnout.

A better strategy is to take regular small breaks throughout the year. In their book *The One Thing*, Gary Keller and Jay Papasan explain that effective entrepreneurs and business people look at the year ahead and book all of their holidays in first, making their time with family and friends a priority.[106] If possible, book leave early and split up the four weeks of entitled leave throughout the year. Remembering to fully switch off while away can help a novice to return to their role feeling refreshed.[107]

Maternity and Paternity Leave

Thirty years ago, a woman who stopped work to have children would likely not have returned to the workforce, or at least not for a decade or more, whereas these days there are more and more physiotherapists going back to work after having children while juggling work and home life. The Australian Government now offers paid maternity leave at minimum wage for up to eighteen weeks to help ease the financial burden.

For dads in Australia, there is two weeks' paid leave available after the birth of their child if they pass a work test and earn under $150,000 a year. This was designed to help support casual employees without annual leave entitlements and self-employed people like tradespeople, small business owners and those working in a family business or farm. While this sounds good in theory, statistics are showing that some new dads are not taking up the offer because of lack of education and understanding about how the scheme works.[108]

It's a positive sign that things have changed and there are flexible roles and more financial support, yet challenges remain for working parents with small children. Increasing costs of childcare (even with the childcare subsidy) make it difficult for families to afford. The average age of first-time mothers is now twenty-eight, which means grandparents are older when their first grandchild is born and are less available for free childcare.[109]

Keeping up-to-date with registration requirements that stipulate twenty hours of Continuing Professional Development (CPD) per annum can be difficult for working parents with reduced incomes. Depending on the type of employment, completing email follow-ups and responding to messages or requests for information in a timely fashion could also be challenging. It's important to mention these trials here so that a career path can be planned with these things in mind. What kind of working arrangements will suit the new graduate when they become a parent? For the mature-age student who already has family commitments, seeking support and feeling empowered to choose the right style of employment can aid job satisfaction.

Personal Leave

Personal leave (which includes sick leave and carer's leave) is something all employees are entitled to. This extends to caring for spouses or former spouses, children, grandparents, parents and stepchildren.

There are some interesting differences in the public system versus the private system. In the public system, people regularly take sick days when they are unwell, perhaps because there is a larger department of staffed physiotherapists to cover. However, in the private system it can be harder to have time off because a long list of private clients will miss out on the help they need if the physiotherapist does not come to work. This can lead to 'soldiering on', which may result in burnout if the physiotherapist needs rest but cannot take it. At times like these, no matter which area of practice the new graduate is in, it is useful to reduce commitments to make health the greatest priority.

It is inevitable that there will be times of illness during one's career. Following the protocol for leave can assist the whole team. This might mean calling in the night before (particularly for an early shift to give adequate time to cancel or shuffle clients), or sending any handover messages to other clinicians in the team (although, ideally, notes should always be organised with a detailed plan so that another clinician can easily come in and take over at any time).

Mental Health Days

Mental health days are becoming increasingly common in the developed world due to increasing work pressures, as reported in a recent study by the World Health Organization which looked at days out of role due to common health and mental problems.[110] The study involved face-to-face interviews with people across twenty-four countries and found that common health conditions such as migraines, cardiovascular disease and mental health disorders made up a large proportion of the reasons for days out of role, and should be addressed to substantially increase overall productivity. Post-traumatic Stress Disorder (PTSD), panic, and Generalised Anxiety Disorder (GAD) were among the top six conditions with highest mean days out of role in all three income groups, which indicated that mental health conditions rank quite high for cause of loss of productivity. Individuals with any disorder had an average of 24.2 more days out of role in a year (31.1 days those with any mental, 24.5 those with any physical) than those with no conditions.

So what does this data mean? It means that there are many people out there suffering with mental health conditions that require them to take time off every once in a while. The milder mental health conditions of GAD and social phobia required fewer days off than PTSD.

It's essential for physiotherapists to feel that they can take time off. All employees need some flexibility and the reassurance that they can have a sick day or mental health day if they require it, or can take a holiday with their family without negative repercussions.

Questions for Self-enquiry

1. Are you currently happy with your remuneration and package as an employee?

2. If self-employed, are you satisfied with current fees and take-home pay at the end of the week?

3. Have you considered your value as a practitioner? What would you ideally like to be paid per hour?

4. Would you consider becoming self-employed once you have gained some experience? Who could you turn to for business mentoring to discuss this?

5. When was the last time you took a holiday?

6. Do you prefer to take all of your time off at once, or do you split it up throughout the year?

7. Have you reviewed the policy for leave requests at your place of work? How much notice do you have to give when taking leave?

8. Have you currently got a holiday booked for yourself? Do you know how much leave you have accrued?

9. How much personal leave have you had to use this year due to your or your child's ill health? How do you feel about that?

10. Have you ever taken a mental health day? Did it help you to feel better?

15
Grief and Loss

All the art of living lies in a fine mingling of letting go and holding on.

Henry Havelock Ellis

Ending a Professional Relationship

Physiotherapists tend to be empathetic people, to varying degrees. There are benefits of this sensitivity, such as being able to sense subtle changes in body language. But there are downsides too, such as becoming emotionally attached and then feeling a sense of separation or loss when a professional relationship ends.

Sometimes a long client relationship ends abruptly because treatment has become ineffective or compromised. At other times the client may only have needed one treatment, perhaps due to being from another city. A physiotherapist may decide to discharge a client or refer them on if their treatment regime has come to an end, or if the physiotherapist feels they can no longer be of service to the client because the condition falls outside of their scope.

At other times, a client may cease therapy without explanation, which can be difficult to understand. The best thing a practitioner can do is follow up and check in, and hope that they will return or at least reply to the contact. Some workplaces have systems in place to set 'recalls' to check on clients. This system can encourage a client to eventually return and to feel supported and cared for, particularly in the case of subsequent injuries.

End-of-life Care

The death of a client is a very different cause for grief. It is a traumatic time for the friends and family of the client, of course, but it can also affect the practitioner who had a professional relationship with the client. For a novice, it can help to debrief – with colleagues, a supervisor, a mentor or even a counsellor, particularly if the loss is affecting clinical practice.

According to the Code of Conduct, good practice primarily involves helping the client to manage their symptoms and concerns in a manner consistent with their values and wishes (which will be different for everyone). This might mean some involvement in palliative care, and always being aware that at any stage, a client can refuse treatment. Effective communication with clients and their caregivers is paramount, as is maintaining professional integrity.

A paper published in the *American Psychological Association Journal* (2013) assessed the psychosocial impact of working in palliative and cancer care on health professionals. In this study, thirty-eight health professionals who provided grief support and counselling in cancer and palliative care (including psychologists, social workers, pastoral carers/chaplains, nurses, group facilitators, and a medical practitioner) each participated in a semi-structured interview. The study identified four themes:

1. **The role of health professionals in supporting people who were experiencing grief and loss issues in the context of cancer**
2. **Ways of working with patients with cancer and their families**
3. **The unique qualities of cancer-related loss and grief experiences**
4. **The emotional demands of the work and associated self-care.**

The study found that health professionals experienced secondary trauma and burnout as a result of their work. This trauma had serious repercussions for their wellbeing and potentially compromised the care they could provide. The findings have implications for the retention of personnel who provide psychosocial care in cancer and the quality and delivery of services for people with cancer and their families. Health professionals are vulnerable to occupational stress, especially those working in 'high-death' contexts.[111]

While there is a need for further research in this area to determine physiotherapists' coping strategies in palliative or cancer care, it can be hypothesised that as caring professionals, working with cancer patients, elderly and frail adults at end-of-life, or intensive-care patients could be distressing.

Recent amendments to the Diagnostic and Statistical Manual of Mental Disorders (DSM-5) highlight what is considered to be 'normal' bereavement in our culture and what is considered to be excessive. When a loved one dies, a full depressive syndrome is a normal reaction to such a loss, with associated symptoms such as poor appetite, weight loss, and insomnia. However, morbid preoccupation with worthlessness, prolonged and marked functional impairment, and marked psychomotor retardation, while uncommon, suggest that the bereavement is complicated by the development of major depression.[112] Though clients are not as close as family members, it is acknowledged that long-term relationships can form, particularly in community and outpatient settings, and it can be challenging when these bonds are broken. Support is available for new graduates feeling emotionally affected by their work. If feeling down or upset for prolonged periods, or suffering from symptoms of depression, a psychologist or counsellor may be of assistance.

Closing a Practice

When relocating or closing a practice, or for the early career physiotherapist who leaves a job to start a business or work elsewhere, good practice involves giving an employer and clients as much notice as possible in accordance with their contract of employment and facilitating arrangements for the ongoing care of current patients. If moving practices or starting a business, it is unethical to 'poach' clients by providing details of the new place of work or encouraging them to leave the practice. This is a breach of the Code of Conduct and there may be repercussions.

Physiotherapists are in a position to develop strong connections with others, but with this privilege can come emotional risk. Whether the end of a professional relationship occurs as a natural result of a resolution of symptoms, or it is forced through conflict, personal choice or even death, a little time, space and gentleness will help the situation to heal.

Questions for Self-enquiry

1. What would you do if one of your clients passed on? Can you think of an appropriate way you could support the family?

2. Do you have a senior practitioner you can seek support from or debrief with (mentor, supervisor) in the event of a disgruntled client who never returns, or the death of a client?

Burnout and Injury

16
Why do Physiotherapists Burn Out?

Our fatigue is often caused not by work, but by worry, frustration and resentment.

Dale Carnegie

What is Burnout?

Burnout is a very important topic for graduate physiotherapists. It is discussed at university, but it can be hard to truly understand until the graduate commences work and experiences the pressures of full-time employment. Not only do physiotherapists need to know what it is, they need to know *why* it happens and the subtleties of this pervasive phenomenon. Being armed with knowledge enables informed decision-making when it comes to the demands of working life.

- What does burnout look and feel like?

- What are the professional and personal costs of burnout?

- How does one find their way back from burnout?

These are questions to be covered in this chapter. But first, what *is* burnout?

Burnout develops when an in individual is exposed to chronic stressors and frustration that exceed their tolerance and mechanisms for coping.[113]

One of the most documented tools (and the gold standard for assessing burnout) is the Maslach Burnout Inventory (MBI). This validated tool was designed by Christina Maslach and her colleague Susan E. Jackson in the early 1980s and consists of twenty-two statements about a person's experiences. Respondents are asked to indicate the frequency at which they encounter these feelings. For example, a statement might be 'I feel used up at the end of a work day' and responses may range from 'never', indicated by a zero, through to 'every day', indicated by a six.

The inventory identifies three distinct categories of chronic stress. According to Maslach, these three categories are sequential and begin with (1) *emotional exhaustion.* As emotional resources are depleted, caregivers feel that they are no longer able to give support at an emotional or psychological level.[114] A sense of prolonged emotional exhaustion leads to the second stage of burnout, known as (2) *depersonalisation,* in which the caregiver is no longer able to empathise with clients during direct care as evidenced by impersonal feelings of detachment, dehumanisation and cynicism towards the recipient of care. The third and final stage of burnout, (3) *reduced personal accomplishment,* is characterised by compromised standards of care and a reduced sense of achievement. By this stage, a healthcare practitioner will be exhibiting signs of decreased professional output and productivity. This can result in dissatisfaction from the client or recipient of care due to the physiotherapist's cynical attitude or withdrawn demeanour, which can further reduce sense of self-efficacy and self-esteem for the physiotherapist.

To give clinical examples of the stages of burnout: emotional exhaustion might be coming home from work and struggling to provide compassion to loved ones, and being moody or impatient due to feeling used up. Depersonalisation might be expressed as cynical remarks or comments about clients, labelling clients as 'difficult' or being unable to empathise with their journey. This behaviour is not appropriate in a clinical setting and requires reframing of the situation to facilitate greater compassion. A sense of reduced accomplishment may manifest as the physiotherapist questioning how much they know and whether they are good enough. This can lead to mistakes, poor attention and a tendency to do 'the bare minimum' and not go the extra mile for a client.

Burnout and Stress

Burnout is closely correlated with stress. The definition of stress within the literature remains elusive, but two traditional models of stress have been proposed: stimulus-based and response-based. The stimulus-based approach identifies certain conditions as stressful, such as workload, time pressure and environmental factors. This is an exogenous model, indicating that the cause of the stress comes from outside of the individual. Conversely, response-based stress is defined by an individual's response (i.e. behavioural, cognitive, and affective) to exposure from a given stressor. This model of stress pertains to stress that is endogenous, or emanating from within the individual.

A third model of stress has been proposed, the transactional model, which holds that stress arises due to the complex interaction between both the environment and the individual.[115] This proposed model deems stress to be 'a mismatch between individuals' perceptions of the demands of the task or situation and their perceptions of the resources for coping with them'.[116] This approach highlights *perception* of stress and ability to cope as being essential to successfully navigating stress in work and life. For example, a new graduate may know their workplace is very busy and that they will likely have back-to-back bookings, and this may be an external source of stress. However, whether the graduate actually feels stressed depends on perception, and taking a different view of the situation can improve the graduate's response to the stressor. Under the right circumstances, feelings of being busy and overwhelmed can instead be converted into motivation to help them achieve their goals and a sense of opportunity for success and prosperity both personally and for the team.

It is important to note that stress and burnout look different for everyone, and can be hard to measure without a standardised tool like the MBI. For some people it might be a repetitive feeling of not wanting to go to work or experiencing morning fatigue. For others it could manifest as exhaustion or feeling emotional. At times, these things may be transient and caused by external factors such as difficult life events. But if they are persistent and the practitioner feels a loss of enthusiasm, it may be a sign of burnout. For some people, life can become a cycle of these feelings. Symptoms may improve at certain times only to resume later. New graduates may find themselves 'pushing through' because there is minimal education and resources available.

Why Are Physiotherapists at Risk of Burnout?

Burnout has been well documented among nurses, doctors, psychologists and counsellors across cultures.[117] [118] [119] While the body of evidence on burnout among physiotherapists is smaller, it is growing, with several recent studies highlighting the specific causes of burnout among physiotherapists (Klappa et al. 2015).[120] Physiotherapists are particularly prone to occupational burnout due to the intense nature of their helping role and constant direct patient care. For new graduates, juggling a new and busy case load, navigating the professional work environment, managing personal issues and understanding their own coping styles can all be sources of stress.[121]

A study from Poland looked at burnout among physiotherapists and the mediating effect of coping styles.[122] Three main coping styles were proposed: (1) *problem-focused coping*, which aims to alter the stressor via a direct action; (2) *emotion-focused coping*, which involves self-preoccupation, fantasy or other conscious activities related to affect regulation; and (3) *avoidance-oriented coping*, which includes seeking out other people (social diversion) or engaging in a substitute task (distraction). Problem-focused coping, which included active decision-making, significantly reduced the level of burnout among physiotherapists. Strategies that were suggested for physiotherapy departments included providing seminars, workshops and social skills training to promote solution-oriented thinking and problem-solving.

The use of emotion-focused strategies was positively correlated with burnout, and it did not appear to be a healthy coping style in the work environment. Individuals who dealt with problems by focusing on associated negative feelings relating to the situation were more likely to develop burnout symptoms. This might be fantasising about vacations or holidays, looking for another job, or ruminating on the undesirable emotions that were felt about a client or client interaction. Therefore, an improvement in emotion regulation could contribute significantly to the reduction of burnout symptoms. This could involve modifying or eliminating the conditions that gave rise to the problem and changing the perception of an experience, a process known as positive reappraisal. Seeking emotional support, acceptance of a situation, and development of spiritual beliefs and practice have also been found to be useful strategies for people with this predominant coping style.[123]

Withdrawal or avoidance coping has also been shown to be associated with poorer mental health outcomes and greater burnout.[124] In a clinical setting, this might look like dissociation, anxious avoidance and escape (including recurrent sick days or sudden unplanned leave).

When one practitioner becomes stressed, it can be easy for others to pick up on that stress or for it to become 'contagious' in the workplace. This phenomenon is known as crossover. A study from the Netherlands explored the interpersonal process that occurs when job stress or psychological strain (stress reactions) experienced by one person affect another person. This paper highlighted that crossover of psychological strains such as anxiety, distress, depression, burnout, adjustment, work-family conflict, and marital dissatisfaction is a real occurrence.[125] It is no surprise that change in a workplace will affect all people involved; people are part of social systems and need to be understood within those systems. The first people to recognise the possibility of crossover of burnout at work were Edelwich and Brodsky (1980), and they stated that 'if burnout affected individuals only in isolation, it would be far less important and far less devastating than it is. Burnout in human services is like an infection in hospitals; it gets around. It spreads from clients to staff, one staff member to another and from staff back to clients.'[126]

Expectations within the workplace may also be a source of stress that can lead to burnout. For example, some private clinics will have Key Performance Indicators (KPIs) displayed and a strong focus on clinician statistics. While this is designed to improve client outcomes and practice outcomes, it can put pressure on staff to perform. However, with the right mentoring and professional development, a new graduate physiotherapist can survive and thrive under all sorts of different working conditions, and this model of clinical practice using KPIs does not need to be feared.

While the traditional perspective of burnout is that it comes from high caseloads and job stress, an alternative viewpoint is that it doesn't necessarily come from overwork.

You don't burn out from going too fast. You burn out from going too slow and getting bored.

Cliff Burton

This notion suggests that burnout can result from a lack of inspiration and career progression. Looking at the way that most private physiotherapists work, there is a lack of structure or framework for how to technically improve or progress through certain levels to feel a sense of achievement in their career. Following this theory, it can be assumed that the solution to burnout is effective professional development, ongoing learning and building passion and inspiration. These topics are covered in detail in Chapter 4.

While physiotherapy may not be the most demanding job in the world, it's not easy either – it can be hard on the mind, and on the hands and body. Physiotherapists need to be mindful about how they are coping – especially new graduates who have so much to learn in those first few novice years. It's important to remember that as difficult as burnout can be on the individual physiotherapist, it affects other people too, including clients and colleagues. Burnout can lead to reduced patient satisfaction, sub-optimal self-reported patient care, and inadequate rehabilitation for patients. Stress has the potential to significantly reduce attention, short-term memory and concentration and may compromise a clinician's decision-making skills. It could even impact on the ability to work hard for and qualify for a job promotion, and have a negative impact on one's career as a result of sub-optimal performance. For the sake of clients and physiotherapists alike, the identification of burnout among physiotherapists, especially new graduates, needs to improve.

Recognising the Signs and Symptoms of Burnout

How does burnout manifest during day-to-day life as a physiotherapist? How can new graduates recognise the signs in themselves and others and take proactive steps to feel better?

Burnout is usually quite insidious and doesn't happen suddenly, so understanding this is key.[127] In the early stages of burnout, one might feel unusually fatigued or tired, with little energy. Insomnia is a sign that things aren't quite right. Perhaps the new graduate may have difficulty falling asleep or staying asleep, with frequent wake-ups during the night. Other common signs are forgetfulness and impaired concentration, and in the later stages, a physiotherapist might feel exhausted, drained and depleted, and may feel a sense of dread about the day ahead.

Physical symptoms of burnout can include heart palpitations, chest pain, shortness of breath, gastrointestinal pain, dizziness, fainting, headaches and nausea. Illness may become more prevalent, with recurrent colds and flus due to a deficient immune system and an increased risk of disease such as chronic fatigue syndrome.[128] Anxiety can present with symptoms of tension and worry, which can interfere with one's ability to perform at work. Depression may be expressed as feeling sad or hopeless about life, and in more serious cases it can lead to thoughts of self-harm. Anger is another serious sign of burnout, and begins as tension and irritability that can escalate into thoughts or acts of violence if unchecked.

Signs that a new graduate is becoming cynical or detached from their work include a loss of enjoyment, pessimism about their clients or workload, and isolation. This can manifest as resisting going out for lunch with colleagues, or consistently closing their door to keep others out. Detachment is the final stage and is a general sense of feeling disconnected from others or from the environment. This might result in calling in sick often, not returning calls or emails, or regularly being late for meetings or appointments.

Signs of ineffectiveness and lack of accomplishment include feelings of apathy and hopelessness about work, that sense of 'what's the point?' Increased irritability can come from feeling ineffective and this can destroy relationships and careers. Lack of productivity, poor performance and chronic stress can prevent the new graduate from feeling like a valuable member of the team.

When any of these signs and symptoms of burnout are identified, it's important to acknowledge them and make a plan to move forward and seek solutions. Having a mentor or someone to be accountable to (whether it's a trusted colleague, mentor, or a counsellor or psychologist) can make all the difference.

Physiotherapists have a remarkable role to play in the lives of others, helping people to heal and recover from injury, and providing tools and resources. The practitioner who suffers repeated bouts of burnout will be unable to continue helping effectively – therefore, it is fundamental to the longevity of the individual practitioner and the profession to explore strategies for identifying burnout, managing it when it occurs, or better still, preventing it from occurring in the first place.

Solutions in Times of Burnout

For physiotherapists currently experiencing severe symptoms of burnout, more urgent measures may need to be taken. These could include:

- Scheduling a meeting with a mentor or employer to discuss challenges and solutions

- Debriefing or problem-solving with a colleague or physiotherapist friend

- Seeking assistance from health professionals. This is especially important, as often when someone is feeling burnt out they have failed to take care of themselves as well as they need to. At such times, the individual must book that doctor's appointment, massage, physiotherapy treatment, or counselling session and allow themselves to be cared for by others.

See Chapter 24 on self-care for further suggestions.

Questions for Self-enquiry

1. Do you understand the signs and symptoms of burnout?
2. Have you ever experienced burnout as a student or physiotherapist?
3. What were the main causes of your burnout?
4. What were the mental and physical signs of burnout that you experienced (if any)?
5. Which area of physiotherapy were you working in when you experienced burnout?
6. What solutions did you draw on?
7. Have you ever noticed clinicians or clients around you experiencing burnout? How did this impact on your own sense of wellbeing (understanding what you now know about crossover)?

17

Why do Physiotherapists Become Injured?

Take care of your body. It's the only place you have to live.

Jim Rohn

Manual Handling and Injury

Physiotherapy students receive a significant amount of manual handling training to help prevent injury to themselves and others. This is imperative because once qualified, the majority of physiotherapists will spend a significant proportion of their working day performing specific manual handling techniques or providing manual therapy. While this provides an excellent opportunity for the physiotherapist to remain fit and active (and in most cases, prevents postural loading from sitting at a desk all day), it also puts physiotherapists at increased risk of injury.

Work-related musculoskeletal injuries among physiotherapists have been explored in a number of studies internationally.[129][130][131][132] An American survey of occupational therapists (OTs) and physical therapists (PTs) found a prevalence rate of 16.5 injuries per 100 full-time OTs, and 16.9 injuries per 100 full-time PTs, a rate similar to workers employed in heavy manufacturing.[133] Another study exploring the prevalence of injuries among physiotherapists in south-east Asian hospitals (2011) found an overall prevalence within a twelve-month period of 71.6%. Female therapists reported a higher prevalence of injuries than males, which was thought to be generally due to smaller stature and disadvantage when transferring patients.[134] Physiotherapists with a BMI greater than 25 reported the highest prevalence of work-related injuries at 80%.

Cromie, Robertson and Best (2000) reported that up to 80% of physiotherapists experienced symptoms of work-related musculoskeletal disorders in at least one body region over a one-year timeframe.[135] The authors also found that over the course of their careers, as many as 91% of physiotherapists will experience a work-related musculoskeletal disorder. The rate of recurrence was as high as 88%.[136] The personal and economic impacts of these conditions are profound. Approximately one in six physiotherapists had reported that a work-related musculoskeletal disorder prompted them to leave the profession or change their area of specialty. Work-related musculoskeletal conditions also carry economic costs to individuals and healthcare organisations that employ physiotherapists through sick leave entitlements, healthcare intervention costs and loss of productivity.[137]

Musculoskeletal injury can take many forms, with previous literature identifying the most common injuries among physiotherapists to be lower back (48%), neck (33%), upper back (23%) and thumb injuries (23%).[138] Physiotherapists can use strategies to minimise the risk of sustaining these injuries (or ease the load if injured) such as modifying the role to include exercise classes instead of only manual therapy, scheduling brief pauses or breaks for snacks, stretches and fresh air, and maximising the use of the equipment available. This may be easier in private practice settings, which can provide access to a gym, rehabilitation equipment, fitballs, theraband and more.

In a hospital setting, it is best to always overestimate the amount of assistance that will be required. There is a 'no lift' policy in all Australian hospitals, and in intensive care units it's often mandatory to have three or four people to help with a bed transfer. As a new graduate, always be confident in asking for help, and ignore any desire to be autonomous when it comes to manual handling. Remember not to catch a falling patient and never manually lift without equipment (such as a stand lifter).

Using what is available can minimise the risk of injury. Monitoring treatment positions of both the client and the practitioner is important; for example, adjusting the bed height and not overworking one joint or maintaining the same position while providing manual therapy. Seeking treatment early on for injuries can help to minimise the impact.

Are Physiotherapists Healthy and Strong?

Physiotherapy is a very physical career, and often those drawn to physiotherapy are already very fit and active. A study that looked at physical activity and health-related quality of life among a small group of young Australian physiotherapists aimed to assess just how healthy and fit recent graduates were. A questionnaire was completed by forty-four physiotherapists from three inpatient units and three ambulatory clinics (with a response rate of 63.7%). Physical activity levels were reported using the Active Australia Survey. Health-related quality of life was examined using the EQ-5D instrument. Results indicated that of this population, the majority were younger than 30 years of age. Almost all respondents exceeded minimum recommended physical activity guidelines (n = 40, 90.9%). Overall, the respondents engaged in more vigorous physical activity (median = 180 minutes) and walking (median = 135 minutes) than moderate exercise (median = 35 minutes) each week. Thirty-seven participants (84.1%) reported no pain or discomfort impacting their health-related quality of life, with most (n = 35, 79.5%) being in full health.[139] This study looked at a small, yet fit and healthy population of physiotherapists. It would be interesting to monitor how well this level of fitness is maintained throughout careers. Further research may be required.

It's useful to acknowledge that injuries can be caused by things outside of the profession too. Normalising injury among physiotherapists and not catastrophising it is very important and should be a strong focus in all practices. Seeking support and getting on with the job are essential at these times where possible, and if need be, the physiotherapist can continue with alternative duties until they have undergone a rehabilitation process. There are many options available.

While injury can be a threat to a physiotherapist's livelihood, it is important to use training and knowledge to do a risk assessment, slow it down and ask for help. Whether injured or not, a physiotherapist can always find ways to continue using their unique skills.

Questions for Self-enquiry

1. Have you ever sustained an injury as a physiotherapist on the job? What did you do to seek support or treatment? If you could go back in time and give yourself some advice as your older and wiser self, how would you handle the situation differently now?

2. Have you ever sustained an injury in your personal life? How might it affect your practice as a physiotherapist?

3. If you were about to perform a technique or transfer and you had a gut feeling that it wasn't safe, what would you do? (Hint: Options could include telling the patient or client that you do not wish to proceed because of safety, speaking to a senior staff member for advice before proceeding, or seeking additional help from another physiotherapist.)

18

Retention: Why do Some Physiotherapists Leave the Profession?

Work is going to fill a large part of your life, and the only way to be truly satisfied is to do what you believe is great work. And the only way to do great work is to love what you do.

Steve Jobs

Physiotherapy Workforce

In September 2015, there were 26,601 physiotherapists registered in Australia (Physiotherapy Career Pathway: White Paper, 2016). This data indicated that of those registered, 89.5% were clinicians, 4.2% administrators, 2.8% educators, 1.5% researchers and 1.9% in other areas. This same workforce data indicated increased numbers of physiotherapists graduating (up 4% from the previous year), with females accounting for most of the growth.

Despite increasing student intakes and graduate numbers, high rates of attrition in the profession (as high as 3.5%) have been flagged as a real concern. In Australia, we are facing a widening gap between the number of qualified professionals and demand for services due to an ageing population.[140,141] A study of new graduates from Curtin University found that as many as 65% of graduates were intent on leaving the profession within ten years, and only 25% predicted a long-term career in physiotherapy.[142]

One solution for this is to increase the numbers of overseas-trained physiotherapists working in Australia, something that has been proposed as the only way to meet Australia's predicted requirements for physiotherapy by 2020. While this is a privilege to have such a diverse population of physiotherapists, it is concerning that we are not able to retain Australian-trained physiotherapists. Can we try to better understand just why physiotherapists are leaving, and help them to stay?

Why Leave?

We have looked at the research regarding potentially low remuneration (Chapter 14) and job satisfaction (Chapter 2) to provide us with answers about why physiotherapists may sometimes choose to move on, possibly seeking a better quality of life and abundance through a different career pathway.

Yet if we look deeper and consider the wise perspective of a mentor, that attrition is the *disease* and burnout or injury are the *symptoms*, it may help us to understand how physiotherapists become so 'ill' that they decide to leave. Burnout and injury can be difficult burdens to carry.

Physiotherapists work so hard to get into physiotherapy, complete their training and continue to learn and strive for success that it is a real shame that they feel they have no other option but to leave and do something else, or have a family and never go back to clinical practice.

If we look closely at injury as a potential cause, we can imagine that a common concern among physiotherapists in the private sector is how they will manage long-term if they have sustained small or large injuries related to professional practice. How will they cope with the pressure of repeated mobilisations and other manual therapy techniques? After some time in the profession, it is only natural that physiotherapists may begin to look for ways to modify their career pathway. It may be hard to imagine doing the same manual work up until the age of seventy (or other retirement age). Realistically, diversifying one's skill set and minimising manual therapy or considering teaching, research or adjunct roles may be strategies to consider for the physiotherapist wanting to remain in the workforce as they age.[143]

A Polish study found that physiotherapists with more than fifteen years of service reported greater satisfaction with physiotherapy as a career than those with less than five years, and those with between five and fifteen years of experience.[144] The more senior clinicians were found to have greater happiness within their professional role and lower reports of burnout than their less-experienced counterparts. The newer physiotherapists were prone to burnout related to reduced job satisfaction and reduced financial status. It was hypothesised that the high level of professional competence required by physiotherapists did not translate into an appropriate salary. The effects of burnout across all groups were ameliorated by satisfaction with work and positive relationships with family and friends.

Cultivating strategies for preventing and managing burnout and injury (covered in Chapter 24), to help physiotherapists make it through those early and middle career years where rates of attrition are highest, could be the best weapon against attrition.

How to Stay and Make it Work

What can a new graduate physiotherapist do if they have that pervasive feeling that they would like to move on from the profession?

Before considering leaving the profession, a physiotherapist must explore all options and make a commitment to keep evolving. For example, if a practitioner is working in Work Health Safety and finding it unsuitable, there are other alternatives including private practice, working with older adults, community rehabilitation, paediatrics, or women's, men's and pelvic health. Areas that are continuing to grow due to technological advances and could be of interest to a budding physiotherapist include pain sciences, neurological physiotherapy and cardiorespiratory physiotherapy.

Physiotherapists that are feeling restless in the profession could look at adding additional therapies to their repertoire, such as acupuncture, Feldenkrais, dry needling, counterstrain, craniosacral or other mind-body medicines. Then there's advanced or extended scope of practice roles – emergency room physiotherapy, prescribing rights and more.

If injury or burnout is an issue, support must be sought so that the physiotherapist can be appropriately rehabilitated and doesn't give up on themselves or their career. While changing pathways can seem like an obvious solution when things aren't working, it can be daunting to change fields completely and it may not always be the right course of action. Sometimes, persistence and resilience-building are better answers. Working through options with a mentor would be wise before taking action.

Physiotherapy as a career can be highly rewarding and prestigious, yet at times may be impacted by injury, burnout and uncertainty. Thankfully, due to the diverse options for changing roles and working environments, anyone can try a new path and remain in the profession with the right attitude and support network. For the new graduate feeling uninspired, be sure to look at the bigger picture and keep searching for answers until the right course of action becomes clear.

Questions for Self-enquiry

1. Have you ever considered leaving the profession? If so, why? Have you discussed this with a mentor or supervisor for support?

2. How many years do you see yourself working as a physiotherapist?

3. At what age have you considered retiring?

4. What strategies can you implement to help you stay in the profession? What areas could you consider for further training or study to keep focused on and inspired by physiotherapy?

The Future Looks Bright: A Progressive Profession

19

Extended/Advanced Scope of Practice and Technological Advancements

Once we accept our limits, we go beyond them.

Albert Einstein

Extended/Advanced Scope of Practice

The terms extended scope of practice (ESP) and advanced scope of practice (ASP) are often used interchangeably in the literature across Australia and internationally. This can create some confusion regarding what they mean.

ESP has been defined as 'a role that is outside the currently recognised scope of practice and one that requires some method of credentialing following additional training, competency development and significant professional experience, as well as legislative change'.[145]

ASP, according to the Australian Physiotherapy Association, refers to 'a role that is within the currently recognised scope of practice for that profession, but that through custom and practice has been performed by other professions. The advanced role may require additional training as well as significant professional experience and competency development.'

A third Western Australian definition of *expanded* scope of practice has been proposed as an umbrella term to encompass both of these.[146] Expanded roles in the UK, Canada, Australia and Ireland may include emergency department physiotherapy, medication prescription or injection, ordering diagnostic testing, military hospitals, paediatric rheumatology clinics and orthopaedic clinics.

A systematic review by Stanhope et al. (2012) looking at hospital outpatient departments in both the UK and Australia reported ESP tasks as injection therapy and removal of plaster of Paris and k-wires. ESP physiotherapists were also permitted to request further investigations such as radiographs and blood tests. Referrals could be made by ESP physiotherapists to other allied health or medical professionals, such as orthopaedic or rheumatology specialists or pain clinics. In some cases, the ESP physiotherapists listed patients for surgery. ESP physiotherapists did not universally have complete autonomy in performing these tasks. Some had to have X-ray requests approved and others had to discuss referrals, surgery listings and requests for radiological investigations with the medical consultants, although the medical consultants were not required to assess the patient. Protocols were developed by physiotherapists to guide examination and assessment, requesting of further investigations and fracture management. The ESP physiotherapists had a variety of training and years of experience – some had Diplomas in injection therapy and over ten years of experience working in musculoskeletal physiotherapy, while others had attained fellowship of the Society of Orthopaedic Medicine.[147]

This review paper found that research into ESP physiotherapy roles in orthopaedics has not considerably improved in quality or volume since the last systematic review was conducted in 2008. There is still no clarity on definitions of ESP roles (sufficient to distinguish them from traditional or advanced practice), and the available research continues to be of lower hierarchy, site-specific, and threatened by bias. The lack of standardised training underpinning ESP physiotherapy practice is evident and there are large differences in autonomy in decision-making. The literature suggests that ESP physiotherapists may be comparable with medical doctors in terms of clinical decision-making pertaining to patients with orthopaedic conditions, and there are indications that ESP physiotherapy services may improve the efficiency of outpatient management pathways for orthopaedic patients.

Extended scope is an exciting and dynamic part of the changing landscape of physiotherapy. With new opportunities emerging all the time, there is plenty of room for the growth of individual clinicians and for the profession as a whole. More research needs to be undertaken to help standardise care.

Virtual Reality, Gaming and Gait Analysis

Virtual reality (VR) is increasingly used in therapy to enhance clinical outcomes. A study from Italy looked at robotics-assisted rehabilitation for the forearm after orthopaedic injuries at the wrist and elbow. The study was of a small sample of ten subjects and involved use of the system called BRANDO for active/passive rehabilitation of the upper limb, through VR exercising gaming scenarios. With this technology, the researchers could explore the possibilities of personalising the exercise's intensity and modifying it manually in a more systematic way than traditional manual physiotherapy (which does have some risks such as overstretching of brachioradialis and the elbow joint). Despite its limitations, the present work greatly contributes to promoting the development of new assisted methods in orthopaedics and further research in this area.[148]

VR has also been touted as useful for those with low back pain, with a small (n=44) randomised controlled trial found to reduce pain and kinesiophobia and improve function in low back pain patients with statistically significant improvements across the Visual Analogue Scale, TAMPA Kinesiophobia Scale, Timed Up and Go and the 6-Minute Walk Test.[149]

Similarly to VR, gaming use has increased in the field of physiotherapy with a study from South Australia assessing the application of an interactive gaming program (Nintendo Wii) in stroke rehabilitation in older adults.[150] The study reported statistically significant differences in Timed Up and Go (TUG) measures in the intervention group, compared to the usual physiotherapy group. We can expect to see an increase in the use of these programs in acute hospitals, rehab centres and residential care facilities as an alternative or adjunct to traditional exercise.

When it comes to advanced technologies, computerised gait analysis (GA) performed in a laboratory equipped with instruments for kinematic, kinetic and EMG data collection is unanimously recognised as the gold standard for objectively assessing human locomotion. This technology has been available for a number of years, but modern technologies are cutting-edge and are clinically useful in paediatrics for assessing before and after management of clubfeet, surgical intervention in cerebral palsy and also for adult stroke rehabilitation. A recent study looking at whether GA aids in clinical decision-making in post-stroke rehab found that it does.[151] GA was found to significantly influence therapeutic planning (both surgical and non-surgical) and reinforce decision-making for chronic post-stroke patients with locomotor disability. It concluded that further work needs to be done to assess the efficacy of GA-based recommendations and to better translate GA results into specific indications for physiotherapists now and in the future.

Lastly, simulation-based training is a notable mention and has become increasingly common as a means of improving confidence among graduate physiotherapists.[152] Simulation involves cases portrayed by professional role-play actors, and the setting, equipment and resources such as medical notes, MRIs and blood tests are prepared to look as authentic as possible. The equipment, environment and interactions with staff, supervisors and colleagues are designed to reflect real-world practice as closely as possible. This approach has been touted as a way to provide novice physiotherapists greater exposure to complex scenarios in a safe learning environment. Students who had completed an immersive simulation placement achieved higher scores in an evaluation of their competence to practice than those who did not complete simulated training. Simulation is also being used by the Australian Physiotherapy Council to conduct assessments of overseas-trained physiotherapists to help them get up to speed with the clinical practice standards in Australia.

The changing landscape of physiotherapy is both exciting and progressive. Keeping well informed of the latest in technological advancements requires diligence, continuing professional development and wider reading.

Questions for Self-enquiry

1. What areas of extended scope of practice would you consider working in?

2. What additional training might you require to be able to practice in extended scope?

3. Who would you speak to if you weren't sure whether what you were doing was within the scope of practice?

4. In what ways could you see VR or gaming benefiting the cohort of patients that you currently work with? Is this an option for rehabilitation in the facility in which you work?

20
Physiotherapist as Coach: Goal-setting with Clients

This one step – choosing a goal and sticking to it – changes everything.

Scott Reed

Physiotherapist as Coach

Physiotherapists are drawn to helping others, and thrive on seeing patients go from illness to wellness. It is easy to become emotionally caught up in a patient's story, but the physiotherapist's role is not to be a psychologist or counsellor. The role of a physiotherapist is to use a motivational approach characterised by open, reflective, empathetic and validating communication to empower clients to make healthy changes.[153] They want clients to feel inspired, to get better and enjoy the journey of recovery.

Physiotherapists are not trained to be health or life coaches, but that is increasingly what the job looks like: supporting people, helping clients to see their own roadblocks and limiting beliefs and transcend them. Coaching has become more popular; the Western diet, overwork and stress mean that people require a lot of commitment and support to exercise, eat well and take care of themselves. Accountability is needed during this process and is one of the reasons why the therapeutic relationship is so important. Being a physiotherapist is so much more than laying hands on, advising the client to drink more water or exercise more. It's about setting targets to help them achieve their goals, providing useful information to help them make informed choices and ultimately fostering a long-term relationship that involves mutual care, respect and trust.

While physiotherapists can feel like they're under a significant amount of time pressure, there is always time for a big smile at the end of a consult to encourage and affirm to the client that they are doing well. It might also mean acknowledging that the client hasn't met their goals; but that's okay, because everyone is a work in progress and can always reassess, refocus and keep moving forward.

While ongoing reassurance and encouragement are excellent examples of extrinsic motivation, the aim of physiotherapy is to provide clients with as many tools as possible so they can self-manage. When faced with a challenge, they will be armed with the strategies to meet it head-on, helping them to develop resilience, confidence and intrinsic motivation.

Goal-setting with the Client

When it's time to set clear goals with a client, one of the best questions to ask is, 'What is this injury stopping you from doing?' This can help to clearly establish the client's greatest difficulty and formulate functional goals based on that deficit. For example, it might be as simple as wanting to sleep through the night without pain on rolling. According to O'Sullivan et al., understanding a client's suffering and functional loss and how this ties in with their beliefs about the condition is an important step towards helping them achieve positive outcomes from rehabilitation.[154]

While goals are important, it's not enough to simply ask a client what their goals are and expect to receive a clear answer. A Swiss article titled 'What do you expect from physiotherapy: A detailed analysis of goal setting in physiotherapy' looked at the fact that healthcare practice guidelines require physiotherapists to include patients in goal-setting. The study analysed patient–physiotherapist consultations and identified how physiotherapists enquired about goals and how patients responded to these enquiries. Thirty-seven consenting patients and their physiotherapists were videotaped during consultation. Conversation analysis was used to transcribe and analyse the data. In eleven cases, physiotherapists enquired explicitly about goals. Patients' responses indicated that problems could arise when physiotherapists expected the patient to have a goal already in mind, and presumed the client had sufficient understanding about 'physiotherapy-relevant' goals. The study concluded that goal-setting is not a straightforward process, and when asking patients to state their goals one must consider that patients might not know what an achievable goal is, or may have social reasons for refraining from telling their physiotherapist about their goals.[155] The results highlighted that in order to promote a partnership, patient-centred approaches are endorsed both in research and in clinical guidelines.

To help refine goals, the physiotherapist must work with the client to determine what they can't yet do but really *want* to do, such as put their pants on without pain, move from sitting to standing without pain, or walk without pain. This way, a specific and functional goal will be determined, rather than just 'I want to feel stronger'.

When goal-setting, it's essential to avoid assumptions about what the client wants. Physiotherapists need to be aware that the patient's goals and the practitioner's goals don't always align, and it's important to have a conversation about this. For example, if a client comes in complaining of neck pain and headaches, but the physiotherapist finds shoulder dysfunction on assessment and treats that without explaining why, the client may feel misunderstood. This can leave the client feeling dissatisfied and disappointed by the end of a session. Ensuring congruency between goals is an important step towards a happier client and an effective therapy session.

It is also important to ensure the client's family and caregiver goals are addressed, if applicable. The physiotherapist may need to speak to the family in the case of treating children or elderly adults. There might be one goal to start with, and when that is achieved another one can be negotiated. This helps to keep therapy moving in the right direction, keeps patients feeling motivated and ensures effective communication.

Setting goals is an excellent way to keep track of progress over time. It is quite common for people to forget just how far they have come and how much they have improved! Keeping clear goals at the front of treatment notes is excellent for boosting self-confidence and self-esteem when these goals are achieved. This is where outcome measures come in – as discussed in Chapter 9, they are a brilliant way to remind everyone involved of progress and improvements, no matter how small. Revisiting goals can also been useful if a client hasn't been adhering to their exercises or has lost motivation. Reminding them of their ambitions and going back to those initial goals can be a powerful way to get clients back on track.

Physiotherapists have an important role as helpers and guides for people. They have the opportunity to inspire from a place of health and keep the motivational approach when things are both good and bad. The physiotherapist might not be there for every step, but can certainly maintain accountability, keep the connection going and be a support person. They can cultivate a relationship that is meaningful, and it needn't be a drain or take up lots of extra time and energy. It's about maintaining a positive attitude and being persistent.

Harold had a special routine for when his clients reached their health goals

Exercise Adherence

Guidelines from the World Health Organization suggest a minimum total of 150 minutes of moderate exercise weekly, combined at least twice weekly with resistance exercises, for adults between the ages of 18 and 64 years.[156] Data from the UK indicates that while around two thirds of those aged 16 and older met physical activity recommendations, this number declined significantly with age.[157]

Exercise prescription is a major component of rehabilitation from injury and subsequently physiotherapy practice. Patient's adherence to such programs is a fundamental part of success of therapy.[158] Barriers to adherence have been found to include poor self-efficacy, fear of pain and inability to fit an exercise program into daily life. A knowledge and understanding of these barriers may help clinicians to (1) identify patients at risk of non-adherence and (2) identify strategies to reduce the effect of those barriers, maximise adherence and improve treatment outcomes.

A systemic review by Jack et al. (2010) found that 14% of patients undergoing physiotherapy did not return for follow-up outpatient appointments, and suggested that non-adherence to treatment and exercise programs could be as high as 70%.[159] Poor adherence was found to compromise treatment outcomes and led to recurrence of symptoms. The study identified ten markers as most important for patients' adherence:

1. **Social support**
2. **Guidance**
3. **Number of exercises (fewer targeted exercises was better)**
4. **Self-motivation**
5. **Self-efficacy**
6. **Previous adherence behaviour**
7. **Low level of physical activity or aerobic capacity at baseline**
8. **Exercise attention**
9. **Worsening of pain during exercises**
10. **High degree of helplessness, depression and anxiety**

These findings highlight the complexity of sticking to a program of exercise – there are so many factors that can influence performance. Physiotherapists can help with each of these factors if they commit and take the time to teach clients how to exercise and explain how the exercise will help them reach their goal. An example of this in clinical practice could be giving a client who is a runner with gluteal tendinopathy very clear instructions and a training load diary, so they can work out the load they are putting on their tissues during their exercises, how much pain it causes them, what the recovery is like and how happy they are with the level of pain they experience (i.e. what can they cope with). This sort of program can help to troubleshoot number (9), the worsening of pain during exercises. This is one reason why some patients stop exercising altogether.

Guiding patients attentively and holistically to address the above factors will ultimately result in better exercise adherence and improved clinical outcomes according to Bachmann C, Oesch and Bachmann S (2018). While clients do need a certain level of self-motivation, and previous experience with exercise certainly appears to help, there is always room for improvement no matter where the client is on their path to wellbeing. A physiotherapist can help support their client to work hard so they ultimately get to where they want to be.

Questions for Self-enquiry

1. Have you ever had a coach or mentor? What are some of the key lessons you learned from the experience or relationship?

2. Do you set goals for yourself? If not, can you start by setting some goals for your health and life for the next three, six, or twelve months? Knowing how to set goals, regularly reviewing them and being accountable to someone else can help you assist other people with their goal-setting.

21
Holistic and Integrative Approaches

The doctor of the future will give no medicine, but will instruct his patients in care of the human frame, in diet and in the cause and prevention of disease.

Sir Thomas Edison

What is Holistic Practice?

During university studies, physiotherapists are trained in the biopsychosocial model. This model is from a Western medicine framework and considers biomedical factors such as disease, disorder and injury, as well as psychological factors such as stress, depression and anxiety and social factors.[160] This model is important as it helps physiotherapists and other healthcare workers to see the bigger picture for the client. However, it is not truly holistic and is potentially still missing some key elements of patient wellbeing. The Eastern medicine framework encompasses a whole body-systems approach, but also looks at more subtle 'elements' of life and how they relate to the human body. It considers the person and their 'constitution' in relation to their illness. This is something that traditional physiotherapists are not trained to do, but this awareness can lead to a much deeper understanding of the client's condition.

A small qualitative research study from the Netherlands by Houben and Mourmens (2014), with arguably limited power but important findings, discussed holism in physiotherapy and compared physiotherapists who were more biomedical in their approach to those who were more holistic. Holism was described as 'a coherent approach of health care instead of the sum of individual techniques'. In other words, the client was to be perceived as a whole, in the community and surroundings where they lived, to help resolve their current ill health. This can only be achieved by looking at the mental, social, emotional and spiritual aspects of the person, not just the physical.[161]

So what can physiotherapists do to practice in a holistic way? Making a commitment to spend just a few minutes during a consult to step outside of the 'normal' physiotherapy paradigm and be a witness to the whole person is being holistic. Sometimes all it takes is stopping to ask a client how they really are – not just on the surface, but underneath. How are they feeling emotionally? What are their hopes and dreams (and are they fulfilling them)? How well are they sleeping? How healthy are their most significant relationships? What are they eating and drinking – are they having enough fresh seasonal fruit and vegetables, or are they self-medicating with alcohol or sugar? What matters most to them and what do they really need from the consult today? (It's not always what the practitioner *thinks* they need.)

In a review article by researcher MG Stineman, she writes: 'I argue that the biomedical and holistic paradigms are not in conflict but rather are both necessary and even complementary.'[162] She discusses a framework that combines them both, called the biopsycho-ecological model, but questions whether implementing such a model in physiotherapy will ever be possible. Potentially yes, provided clinicians have adequate training and time to provide a more in-depth subjective examination.

It's important to note that the ability to practice in a holistic way can be greatly impacted by the working environment. For example, in the hospital setting it can be hard to be holistic when the reductionist approach is all-pervasive. The notion that patients have a doctor for this part of the body, a surgeon for that one, a physiotherapist for the muscles and a dietitian for the food is useful, as practitioners all have different roles to play in the recovery process, but it can be difficult to create the sense of cohesion that a client really needs. Short consults in private practice can also prohibit the real connection that may occur in a longer session where deeper layers of a patient's condition and personal situation can be revealed.

Acupuncture in Physiotherapy

Acupuncture is a holistic approach to patient care that is now found within the physiotherapy profession. It is an ancient pain relieving modality; one of the principal techniques of traditional Chinese medicine (TCM) and has been recognised by the World Health Organization (WHO, 2002) as an effective therapy for a variety of conditions. A Spanish literature review looked at the use of acupuncture among health professionals and found a growing interest in the study, practice and recommendation of acupuncture among health professionals and medical students in countries such as

Austria, Germany, Australia and the UK.[163] Some of the reasons people sought acupuncture included:

- Lack of response to conventional treatment
- Absence of available or appropriate treatment
- Perceived lack of adverse effects of acupuncture
- Patient preference
- Belief in its efficacy and existence of documented evidence.

Within the review, health professionals agreed that the holistic approach of acupuncture allowed them to treat the whole person (the totality is more than the sum of its parts) in opposition to conventional medicine, which is purely focused on symptoms. As a consequence, some participants considered that they treated a person and not a patient. They also found that they were focused on the healing process, self-care and lifestyle.

In another study, 800 acupuncture practitioners were selected by computer-generated randomisation sequences from four major UK-based professional associations. Of those 800 participants, 29% were physiotherapists who practised acupuncture. The study found that patients most commonly consulted for low back, neck, shoulder and knee pain, as well as headaches and migraine. Treatment for infertility by independent acupuncturists was found to have increased fivefold in ten years. The trial concluded that acupuncture was a substantial contribution to healthcare in the UK, with an estimated four million sessions provided annually.[164]

It's important to differentiate acupuncture from dry needling. Dry needling is used to treat myofascial trigger points for pain reduction, whereas acupuncture is based on the idea that living beings have an inner energy known as Qi (pronounced 'chee'), and it is the flow of this inner energy (as well as blood and body fluids including lymph) that sustains them.[165,166] According to TCM, balanced Qi and body fluid movement are vital to good health, and illness and disease are caused by imbalance or stagnation. A TCM approach also considers warmth, coolness, hardness, softness, moisture and dryness in the tissues of the body. Balancing these attributes is an important part of the treatment process. An increasing number of studies indicate that acupuncture also has an effect on the autonomic nervous system and functions including blood pressure, pupil size, skin conductance, skin temperature, heart rate, pulse rate and even heart rate variability.[167]

From a more Western perspective, other ways in which acupuncture might affect the body include the pain-gate theory and endorphin-release model.

Undertaking additional training in either integrative acupuncture or dry needling is becoming increasingly common among physiotherapists. It is wise for the new graduate to consider which approach to treatment resonates with them before commencing professional development. Seek support from a mentor and do plenty of research before making this decision.

Complementary Medicine

Complementary medicine (CM) includes a variety of practices and therapeutic products developed outside of mainstream Western medicine such as homeopathy, Ayurveda, naturopathy, meditation and, as previously mentioned, acupuncture. How well do physiotherapists understand what these modalities are? Can they identify when a client would benefit from referral to a nutritionist (versus a dietitian), naturopath or other CM practitioner?

Two Australian studies looked at the referral patterns of doctors, registered nurses, and allied health therapists in the area of maternity care and found that these professions did not generally refer patients for complementary and alternative medicine because of a lack of personal knowledge on the subject.[168] [169] Other reasons for lack of referral included not knowing a suitable CM practitioner and thinking it was not necessary. The research concluded that further education for healthcare professionals about CM may help to integrate CM into mainstream care. The study found that when it came to the area of maternity care, greater communication, respect and co-operation among all health practitioners was needed to understand the dynamics that affect providers' decisions to use or refer to CM practitioners for maternity care.

In Australia there has been a climate of distrust towards CM, reflected by changes to the national health insurance providers and a removal of rebates for a number of CM therapies in 2019.[170] These included, but were not limited to, naturopathy, homeopathy, yoga, Feldenkrais, and Pilates. The reason for these changes was perceived lack of evidence-based practice. This may change again in future, depending on government, and particularly if research can continue to be undertaken to substantiate the efficacy of natural therapies.

There is limited research into the use of CM among physiotherapists, but anecdotally there is a trend towards greater awareness, with some private clinics promoting sale of supplements including magnesium.[171] As more physiotherapists use holistic approaches and integrate complementary medicine, it's important they cover themselves with adequate insurance and registration, and maintain professionalism and integrity at all times. CM may well become the next extended/advanced scope of practice, paving the way for physiotherapists to treat the whole person, taking into account diet and lifestyle, sleep and stress to further enhance the health promotion focus that physiotherapists already have.

Wanda found integrating natural therapies into physiotherapy challenging when the plants refused to stretch

For physiotherapists that are practising more holistically, it may feel isolating at times being far away from mainstream practice. This can be highlighted when attending professional development courses or events or if treating referred compensable clients. Having to explain to other health professionals a different mode of operation (perhaps longer appointment times) may be difficult. Connecting with like-minded practitioners and having a clear message regarding services offered (and communicating this well to third parties) is essential.

For the new graduate who feels inspired to learn more about CM, it may be worth considering formal or informal qualifications in a CM field. Speaking to a mentor can help to clarify these life-changing decisions, but the ultimate decision will always lie with the individual.

Physiotherapists have a responsibility to help clients to the best of their ability and ensure that they are looking at the whole person. All it takes is a commitment to spend a few minutes of a session asking the right questions and delving a little deeper to better understand the client's needs, which may include referring for treatment that will be complementary to their physiotherapy care.

Questions for Self-enquiry

1. What does the term 'holistic' mean to you?

2. In what ways can you be more holistic in your approach with your clients?

3. What additional professional development training would you like to do as a physiotherapist to help you become more well-rounded in your patient care?

4. What do you feel are current barriers in clinical practice to being more holistic? What could you do differently to think about the bigger picture for clients?

Caring for the Self and Others

22
Mindfulness for Physiotherapists

Feelings come and go like clouds in a windy sky.
Conscious breathing is my anchor.

Thich Nhat Hanh

What is Mindfulness?

Mindfulness has been described as 'the quality or state of being conscious or aware of something'.[172] Mindfulness is a mental state achieved by focusing one's awareness on the present moment while calmly acknowledging and accepting one's feelings, thoughts, and sensations. It's commonly used as a therapeutic technique, and more people are becoming aware of this technique for harnessing the mind and improving wellbeing.

It may be particularly useful for physiotherapists to cultivate mindfulness, as the demands they face at work include heavy caseloads, limited control over their work environment, long hours and pressure to maintain clinical competency.

The benefits of incorporating mindfulness into practice are immense. Moments of stillness and breathing can help one to cope with the demands of life and clinical practice. Meditation becomes a means of self-care and burnout prevention. It can also help to ensure that the physiotherapist is grounded and cultivating the right mindset before starting a treatment session. Meditation teaches checking-in with the self and breathing during sessions with clients. Over time this can be learned in the car, at home and with friends.

So often clients are taught to breathe well – it's wise for physiotherapists to take their own advice and lead by example.

"Sorry, he's running a bit behind today..."

A study from Australia titled 'Head, heart and hands: Creating mindful dialogues in community-based physiotherapy' explored the experiences of five physiotherapists and their 'family care teams' (eight family members and five carers). Analysis of the data from interviews and a focus group revealed that these relationships evolved as the clients, families and carers allowed their physiotherapists to learn about them and subtly welcome them into their home, otherwise labelled by one participant as their 'sacred space'. Building trust and connection, feeling a sense of non-judgement, and making the most of the therapeutic care provided were important to the clients. Mindful and responsive connection is vital to enhance communication with clients and is something that could be explored further in undergraduate and continuing physiotherapy education.[173]

Simple Mindfulness Techniques for Practitioners

Breathing meditation can be used to anchor the breath to the body. When too much time is spent in the mind, it is easy to forget to tune into the body and connect with what the body needs (for example, food or rest).

Body scan meditation is a form of autogenic relaxation, and involves mentally scanning the body from head to toe and encouraging relaxation of all muscle groups progressively. It can be used to reduce muscle tension and to help facilitate physiological relaxation and parasympathetic nervous system activity.

Nature meditation can be performed as easily as sitting outside and mindfully observing the breath and surroundings. It can be very calming to be present with the flowers, the breeze, the sun or the sand underfoot without trying to 'be' somewhere else mentally, without checking a device such as a phone. Taking time each day and during work hours to be in nature, weather permitting, is an excellent way to reconnect and reduce stress.

Walking meditation can be performed on the way to a meeting, while walking to the car, or even travelling down the hallway in the workplace. In its most diligent form, it involves slowing the act of walking down considerably so that the meditator focuses on the infinitesimal parts of the sequence of movement and thinks the following: lifting, lifting, lifting; moving, moving, moving; heel down, mid foot down, toes down, etc. – then repeat with the other foot.

Guided meditation can be performed by listening to another person read aloud a meditation. This is useful for relaxing and unwinding, for using at home or even in bed if the intention is to sleep. There are many guided meditation apps available and video tutorials online.

Sound meditation and chanting involves the use of musical instruments, singing bowls, chimes and others, sometimes called 'sound baths', as the body is immersed in the vibration of sound. Chanting can be used to still the busy mind and help bring a sense of calm. Popular things to chant include mantras such as 'om' (the universal sound meaning 'we are all one'), or 'peace' or 'love'.

Prayer is also an important part of daily life for many people, whether in a church or while at work or on the bus. Having a connection with others and with a higher power can help some people to see the bigger picture of their life and be a source of great comfort and joy.

Questions for Self-enquiry

1. What do you do for relaxation? Have you ever tried mindfulness-based stress reduction (MBSR) techniques?

2. What do you feel in your body when you are stressed? Is there a specific area where you experience discomfort or tissue tightening?

3. What 'worry thoughts' do you commonly find yourself having throughout the day?

4. Have you ever attended or participated in a formal meditation session?

5. Does prayer or awareness of a higher power bring meaning to your day?

23
Building Resilience

Joy, collected over time, fuels resilience – ensuring we'll have reservoirs of emotional strength when bad things do happen.

Brené Brown

What is Resilience?

Resilience is a term used to describe the way in which individuals rise above and overcome adversity. The word resilience originates from the Latin 'resiliere' meaning to 'jump back' which explains the colloquial term of 'bouncing back from adversity'.[174] Resilience involves recovering from trauma or life problems and returning to baseline health and wellbeing, although the path to achieving this is different for everyone.

Resilience has increasingly been identified in international literature as a desirable characteristic for health professionals. Teaching students how to cultivate these qualities during their undergraduate programs has gained traction, although in practice, teaching resilience may be challenging, as there are so many contextual and individual factors at play.

Resilience Among Students

A study by Delany et al. (2015) looked at resilience-building among students as a method of coping with the challenges of clinical placement. Poor resilience in clinical placements due to anxiety and reduced coping strategies has been found to interfere with learning, performance and the ability to provide adequate care for patients. The researchers developed a resilience program to use with students which involved Cognitive Behavioural Therapy (CBT) and strengths-based therapy to monitor behaviour and create the desired change among students. The CBT component focused on building students' awareness and teaching skills to reduce distress, and learning to use cognitive control to optimise their learning and clinical outcomes. Resilience strategies included (but were not limited to) dialogue rehearsal for learning scenarios, controlled breathing, time management, increasing pleasurable activities and appropriate exercise/diet, monitoring self-talk, increasing mindfulness, developing coping strategies based on strengths and past achievements and logging achievements. The results of the study were positive and students found that replacing stressful challenges with positive coping strategies was a potentially powerful tool to help build self-efficacy and cognitive control as well as greater self-awareness.[175]

While stress may be prevalent for some, it's up to the individual to make the best of the situation. It won't be long before the physiotherapist enters the workforce, with its own unique challenges and demands. Life as a student is a precious time of reduced responsibility and phenomenal learning that ought to be embraced and celebrated while it lasts.

Building Resilience and Thriving in Clinical Practice

The new graduate physiotherapist will have many experiences in those first few years – some failures as well as successes. Accepting that both will be guaranteed parts of life as a physiotherapist can help the new graduate celebrate their 'wins' and acknowledge their mistakes without clinging to either as they commence clinical practice. A useful motto for clinical practice is 'this too shall pass'. Indeed, all things will pass, both good and bad. Learning not to lament mistakes but instead to make them right, debrief and move on is an important mark of maturity as a practitioner.

Personal and professional challenges can arise for novices and experienced physiotherapists alike, and it is at these times that practitioners can draw on the support networks around them, both personal and professional, and dig deep to process the trauma or difficulty in their own time and way. At such times, clearly having one's core values in mind (discussed further in Chapter 25) and utilising strategies for self-care (Chapter 24) can help a physiotherapist to feel aligned despite the difficult event and recover better.

To thrive as a physiotherapist, it helps to understand the meaning of the word 'thrive', which is to 'grow well or vigorously'. It can also mean to prosper or flourish, which is exactly what we ultimately desire as physiotherapists and human beings.[176] It can be difficult to constantly thrive, just like the earth has its time for sowing seeds and its time for harvest, and the moon waxes and wanes, we too will experience the ups and downs of life, the light and shadow, times of growth and times of integration. An important revelation for the new graduate is to come to a place of peace with where they are on their journey, knowing that they may not always be 100% happy, and that everything may not always go well each day. But if they trust the path that is unfolding, and commit to doing their best in the moment, they will be able to look forward with hope, and one day look backwards with wisdom, knowing that they were heading in the right direction all along.

Questions for Self-enquiry

1. Can you think of any times during your life as a student or young professional when you had to cultivate resilience? What did that look like for you?

2. What does the word 'thrive' mean to you?

3. Can you remember times when you felt you were thriving in work or study? Which specific tasks or life circumstances made you feel this way?

24
Self-care for Physiotherapists

Rest and self-care are so important. When you take time to replenish your spirit, it allows you to serve others from the overflow. You cannot serve from an empty vessel.

Eleanor Brownn

What is Self-care?

Firstly, what is self-care? This term has been defined as activities performed with the intention of improving or restoring health and wellbeing for oneself, as well as treating or preventing disease. Self-care involves the general health decisions that most of us make about exercise, healthy eating, good hygiene, self-medication, and avoiding health risks such as smoking and excessive drinking. At times it might also involve taking care of minor ailments, long-term conditions and seeking rehabilitation when required. Individuals perform self-care alone or with support from their next of kin or professionals such as service and healthcare providers.[177]

It's important to realise that self-care doesn't always mean going to a yoga class or for a run. While physical activity is very important, sometimes what is really needed is to rest, nap or go to bed early. Learning to practice self-enquiry throughout the day and making sure that small needs are being met over time can make a big difference to wellbeing by the end of the week.

Why Do Physiotherapists Need Self-care?

Self-care can be hypothesised as a tangible thing, a set of practices that the practitioner performs to optimise their own wellbeing and reduce signs and symptoms of burnout in an ongoing, preventative approach. The challenge is to care for the self as much as others. Self-care can't be reserved just for the weekends or days off; it needs to be an integral part of how work and life are organised. It might mean taking time out to have a nice lunch in the park and stepping away from the computer or office, exercising regularly and being generally healthy to prevent risk of musculoskeletal injury in the workplace.

Physiotherapists spend the bulk of their professional lives with the wellbeing of others in the forefront of their minds. Not only does the professional helper lend an ear to their patient, place hands on and gently guide them on the path to healing, they also invest significant amounts of time out of work hours improving their knowledge base and technical skills so they can devote their time to helping others.

It is therefore essential for the clinician to take exceptional care of themselves so that this caring for others can be as effective as possible and can come from a healthy place. Any self-care that a practitioner undertakes can be seen as prevention or future-proofing oneself against burnout. It is much easier to keep burnout at bay than it is to go through the recovery process.

Food, Sleep and Feeling Good

To help prevent burnout, it can be useful for the practitioner to make a list of their needs in a week. Some things might be non-negotiable, such as having seven to eight hours of sleep a night. However, with young children in the house this might not always be possible. Understanding that food can be medicine and knowing which foods help to increase energy and which foods do the opposite can be extremely important, particularly on busy days at work. Too much alcohol, sugar, caffeine and highly processed foods can deplete the body and reduce immunity. Increasing dietary intake of fruits and vegetables, lean protein sources, nuts, seeds and fruits can make a big difference to how one feels and how effective they can be at work.

When injury or aches and pains occur, seek advice from another practitioner – whether it's a massage therapist, physiotherapist, or chiropractor – to receive the right treatment and get well as quickly as possible. Noticing any patterns of burnout or stress is important – for example, it can be common for practitioners to burn out around the same time each year. The transition from autumn to winter can be particularly taxing for some as the cold and flu season begins. At these times of the year, it is vital to take extra care to keep warm, keep moving, eat nourishing foods, drink plenty of water and get enough sleep. Becoming more self-aware as a practitioner sets a good example for clients to follow.

Keeping fit, eating a balanced diet and embodying work–life balance can help a novice to be their best in those early years, which will create a positive foundation moving forward. It's important to acknowledge that there is no such thing as a perfect practitioner, and all human beings have their flaws. The challenge is having patience and understanding these innate flaws while still doing one's best to provide optimum patient care. It's not easy balancing health, work, and personal life, and it is a job that will always be there, no matter which stage of the career path someone is at.

Shiva, The Physio

For the novice, it can be useful to workshop some strategies so that when work and life become busy, there is a safety net in place to help reset the balance again. Making a list of the things that help to foster wellbeing (such as walks on the beach) and then a list of things that are energy-zapping (such as chronic repeated checking of social media or emails) can be a useful exercise. There is a whole body of research now demonstrating the link between phone use and blue screens and increased anxiety and depression. Leaving the phone out of the bedroom and avoiding screens as much as possible during the day and before bed can make a big difference to focus, happiness and wellbeing. If screens cannot be avoided, taking regular breaks and having time outside in the fresh air can be recharging.[178]

For the new graduate, strategies might include exercising before or after work, making time for meal preparation, attending meditation classes, practising yoga, or receiving massage, chiropractics, physiotherapy, acupuncture or other hands-on body work. Seeking support from a medical practitioner for management of any pre-existing conditions and for regular blood tests as part of a general check-up is important, as is booking a time with a counsellor or psychologist if the physiotherapist needs a supportive person (other than family or friends) to talk things through. Natural remedies can also be used to aid wellbeing in the workplace, including essential oils and supplements. A naturopath can assist with correct prescription of supplements based on deficiency and can help to treat a range of conditions from stress and anxiety, to gastrointestinal dysfunction, fertility issues, hormonal imbalance and more. A nutritionist or dietitian can assist with dietary requirements and special diets if food intolerance or weight gain require intervention.

Radical Self-care

For the novice already feeling flat, low or burnt out, it may be time for some radical self-care. While taking time off may seem like the obvious first response, a sudden holiday is often not realistic.

If we look at the example of a sports physiotherapy environment, physiotherapists don't often tell their injured or burnt out clients to stop their vocation. In fact, stopping is rarely an option. Instead, they modify the client's training load until they feel back on track or their pain eases and they can do more. The same can be said for the physiotherapist who is burnt out or injured. Stopping completely is rarely an option, and becoming completely burnt out or seriously injured to the point where work is not possible is an unfortunate outcome that can impact greatly on the team and clients as well as the individual. Even though quitting might feel like a good option, considering a more structured, long-term approach or exit strategy may be required.

New research from Maslach and Leiter (2017) contains a few useful suggestions.[179] The paper focuses on medical physicians, but the insights can be extrapolated to physiotherapy or other caring professions.

Maslach and Leiter identified four key steps to alleviate burnout:

1. **Know the problem (understand and accept burnout and what it feels like)**

2. **Enhance a teamwork perspective (and actively foster communication)**

3. **Build a culture of appreciation (practise gratitude explicitly and regularly)**

4. Realistic recovery (ensuring adequate time for practitioners to rest and recharge).

Hard times will happen throughout life and in these times, radical self-care may be required. The new graduate must learn to see the warning signs of burnout and use the key steps discussed to remedy the situation. In the words of author Bryce Courtenay:

'If you're going to add value to yourself you must make yourself the top priority. You are, after all, the most urgent project you can possibly undertake. Working on yourself is the single most rewarding thing you can do. Eventually someone will benefit hugely from the result.'

Questions for Self-enquiry

1. What self-care practices do you engage in at home and at work?

2. Do you take time for regular breaks throughout the day? Make note of how long your breaks are and be sure to stop for morning tea, lunch and afternoon tea to pause and take care of yourself with healthy food, fresh air and exercise.

3. List three self-care practices or nurturing rituals that you could add to your life.

4. Consider starting a list of the things that 'light you up'. Keep it somewhere prominent at home or work so that you can refer to it daily and choose activities that support keeping fit, eating well and feeling good. Also consider a list of what brings you down so that you are aware of your triggers.

5. Have you ever practised radical self-care at short notice?

6. Have you ever put self-care in your diary at the start of the week to make it a priority?

25
Community Care and Philanthropy

If you're in the luckiest 1% of humanity, you owe it to the rest of humanity to think about the other 99%.

Warren Buffett

What is Community Care?

Community is defined as 'a set of individuals with shared values, assumptions and beliefs, whose interests, whether material or ideological, are bound together'.[180] Communities bind individuals into a collective whole. To be part of a community, one must gain 'admission' and demonstrate a commitment to the wellbeing of the collective. Physiotherapists are almost always part of a community, whether that is an organisation or a private business or enterprise. Physiotherapists are leaders in the field of health and wellbeing, and people look to them for direction and education. Being informed about health policy reforms and the latest in research and disseminating that information can help to build trust within communities.

Self-care versus Community Care

It's important to acknowledge that our highly individualised society can over-emphasise self-care. While self-care is an effective way for physiotherapists to ensure they are well fed, have slept adequately and have made time for their passions, it's not enough to simply focus on that. The reality is that the communities physiotherapists work in *need* them to be well and thriving so they can care and contribute wholeheartedly.

For the novice starting out in clinical practice, it can be useful to consider which community groups they would most like to be involved in and support. This support could be more formal as part of employment or volunteering, or it could be more personal, such as with a church group, sporting club or non-government organisation. Supporting friends and family and building a community in one's own personal life are equally important. Joining your professional association can also help to build a sense of community as you grow into your professional role.

Discovering Passion

Passion has been defined as 'a strong inclination toward a self-defining activity that people like (or even love), find important, and in which they invest time and energy on a regular basis'.[181] Personal passion has been discussed, but what about professional passion? How can these be harnessed by physiotherapists in order to feel inspired and continue to grow?

Two types of passion – harmonious passion and obsessive passion – were looked at in a review paper that followed a cohort of nurses. Harmonious passion involved being passionately engaged with the work, enjoying it while performing it, and being able to stop the task at any time and wilfully and happily return to life. Obsessive passion, by contrast, was characterised by a controlled internalisation of the activity into one's identity and self. This type involved strong feelings of being attached to the activity, such as social acceptance or self-esteem. The nurses who were obsessively passionate about their work experienced greater burnout because of the psychological conflict it induced between work and other life activities. There was also a lack of job satisfaction for these nurses, who were relying on work for their sense of identity. On the other hand, harmonious passion and being able to let go and get on with other things prevented the experience of conflict and contributed to job satisfaction, thereby protecting the nurses from work-related burnout.

How can physiotherapists learn from this and be passionate about the work they do, without taking it home? This is perhaps one of the greatest challenges for the highly passionate, committed physiotherapist.

Identifying Core Values

Discovering the values that lie at the very core of oneself is equally as important as identifying and embracing life goals and passions. Core values are principles or beliefs that are significant to the individual and something that they are not willing to compromise on. Values such as integrity, honesty, generosity, modesty, kindness, compassion and health are highly esteemed.

Often, integrity is a pivotal part of clinical practice and means that the practitioner's actions and words align. This involves being reliable and following through on what has been promised and truly 'walking the talk'. A good moral code to follow is also to 'under-promise and over-deliver' as this shows clients that you really do care, and is much better than doing the opposite.

The result of embracing positive core values can lead to good deeds and genuine care and concern for others. These values can be drawn on in times of need to help make decisions, to align to one's life purpose and ultimately to care better for communities, families, friends and clients.

Philanthropy

Entrepreneurial philanthropy involves the pursuit of big social objectives on a not-for-profit basis through active investment of economic, cultural, social and other resources. Entrepreneurial philanthropists, by extension, tend to have a desire to accumulate significant personal wealth, a large share of which they then choose to assign to philanthropic activities.[182] Physiotherapists have the power to accumulate wealth through business or personal endeavours. They can then choose what to do with that wealth and whether to reinvest in their business, or tithe money to the charities or causes they would like to support. For example, if the environment is a personal passion, investing in sustainable companies and businesses is a step closer to achieving personal integrity, and helping the planet.

For the physiotherapist who has dreams of working or travelling abroad, considering ways to work for a paid or voluntary organisation that has the same values could help to make it a meaningful experience. Bringing this experience back from overseas is one way to help local communities in Australia, as physiotherapists return with expertise and knowledge. Some new graduates are drawn to volunteer in places that align with their values, such as a hospital. Not-for-profit organisations such as Australian Volunteers International (AVI) can help to support recent graduates in finding a role. Spending time working in Australia before heading overseas is a wise consideration and will help the new graduate to gain experience they can use while they travel, and increase the likelihood of a successful application (many of these organisations have a minimum requirement of experience). Thinking just that little bit bigger can help the physiotherapist to reach outside of their comfort zone; the most successful people, companies and wellness leaders always do.

Questions for Self-enquiry

1. Are you currently involved in the health and wellbeing of one or more communities?

2. What are you passionate about? Make a list of work-related passions and personal passions. Identify ways to prioritise them in your life, without making work passions more important than personal passions.

3. Make a list of the top five core values that you resonate most strongly with. Next to each one, write a sentence to describe what this value means to you.

4. If you had all the money and time in the world, which charities or organisations would you support and why? Consider small ways that you can contribute, or pledge to contribute, even small amounts of money, time or expertise.

5. If you were to 'mind map' your journey as a physiotherapist, what would it look like? Create a mind map of the clinical areas you would like to experience.

6. Lastly, but of great importance – what is the meaning of life? What is your life's greatest purpose?

Afterword

The Journey

The first few years of clinical practice are indeed an epic journey, full of adventure, challenges and opportunities. When you finally become a physiotherapist, there is a deep sense of achievement and excitement for what lies ahead. Every experience you've had during your undergraduate degree (and life) up until now will shape you into the practitioner that you will become. You will find that your journey and the journeys of your colleagues and clients will merge as you grow as a practitioner, and discover that all of our paths are intertwined in some way, whether it's fleeting or over many years.

Within these pages you've hopefully felt the comfort of a community and can trust that you are never alone, as budding physiotherapists all over the world are experiencing similar doubts or worries. Know that things will unfold as they need to, and that you will do the best you can with the knowledge you have right now. Taking care of yourself is an essential part of the journey, but in this busy world, keeping the balance is not always easy. It sets a good example for our clients if we can care for ourselves and truly be the change we wish to see in the world.

You've now learned a range of tools and tips to help you prevent injury and burnout and to ultimately thrive in your first few years in clinical practice. Remember to harness these tools and seek mentoring support if you need further clarification to help you choose your path. There are no short-cuts and it will be hard at times, but it will be worth it in the end. Commit to professional development that interests you, keep things simple if you're feeling overwhelmed, and take the journey one step at a time. Remember that some struggles and 'growing pains' are a natural part of the process.

You can come back to this book at any time for comfort and peace of mind. The questions for self-enquiry provide excellent opportunities to workshop situations if you're feeling lost or confused.

I wish you well on the road to success and happiness as a physiotherapist. Remember that you *always* have options and support and it's never too late to reinvent yourself.

Connect with Elizabeth

For more support in finding your unique career path, visit Elizabeth's website at elizabethsantos.com.au for articles, events and one-to-one as well as group mentoring services.

You'll also find her on social media at 'Whole Living with Elizabeth Santos':

instagram.com/wholelivingelizabethsantos

www.facebook.com/wholelivingwithelizabethsantos

twitter.com/whole_living_

About the Author

Yesterday I was clever so I wanted to change the world. Today I am wise, so I am changing myself.

Rumi

Elizabeth lives in the Adelaide Hills with her husband Ricardo and son Leonardo. As a family they often explore the countryside, visit family or friends and enjoy the relaxed lifestyle that Adelaide affords.

Elizabeth graduated with a Bachelor of Physiotherapy from the University of South Australia in 2006. After becoming injured and burnt out as a new graduate physiotherapist in 2008, Elizabeth sought many modalities to help her recover, including natural therapies. She continued to work as a physiotherapist, predominantly in private practice, and went on to study a Bachelor of Health Sciences majoring in nutrition, naturopathy and Western herbalism at Endeavour College of Natural Health.

After the birth of her son in 2015, Elizabeth developed a passion for working in maternity healthcare and continues to undertake further professional education in this area. She practises as both a physiotherapist and naturopath in private practice in Adelaide.

About the Author

This book is the culmination of decades spent on a quest of personal and professional development. Elizabeth believes that when we practise good self-care, we can better connect with our community and be of greatest service to others.

You can meet Elizabeth by attending one of her workshops or talks where she teaches the importance of self-care and community care to sustain mental, emotional and physical wellbeing. These talks encourage the prevention of and recovery from burnout for helpers, teachers, health professionals and carers. Elizabeth also offers one-to-one and group mentoring for new and recent graduates.

Please email info@elizabethsantos.com.au to share your thoughts, comments and questions as you work through the 'Questions for Self-enquiry.' For details of Elizabeth's events, mentoring and more visit

elizabethsantos.com.au

Bibliography

1	McIntyre, J & Naylor, S 2010, 'Are physiotherapy students adequately prepared to successfully gain employment?' *Physiotherapy*, vol. 96, no. 2, pp.169-175.

2	Pera, R, Viglia, G & Furlan, R 2016, 'Who am I? How compelling self-storytelling builds digital personal reputation', *Journal of Interactive Marketing*, vol. 35, pp. 44-55.

3	Edmiston, D 2014, 'Creating a personal competitive advantage by developing a professional online presence', *Marketing Education Review*, vol. 24, no. 1, pp. 21-24.

4	Atkinson, R & McElroy, T 2016, 'Preparedness for physiotherapy in private practice: Novices identify key factors in an interpretive description study', *Manual Therapy*, vol. 22, pp. 116-121.

5	Adam, K, Peters, S & Chipchase, L 2013, 'Knowledge, skills and professional behaviours required by occupational therapist and physiotherapist beginning practitioners in work-related practice: A systematic review', *Australian Occupational Therapy Journal*, vol. 60, no. 2, pp. 76-84.

6	McMahon, S, O'Donoghue, G, Doody, C, O'Neill, G, Barrett, T & Cusack, T 2016, 'Standing on the precipice: Evaluating final-year physiotherapy students' perspectives of their curriculum as preparation for primary health care practice', *Physiotherapy Canada*, vol. 68, no. 2, pp. 188-196.

7	Hammond, R, Cross, V & Moore, A 2016, 'The construction of professional identity by physiotherapists: A qualitative study', *Physiotherapy*, vol. 102, no. 1, pp.71-77.

8	Bosch, B & Mansell, H 2015, 'Interprofessional collaboration in health care: Lessons to be learned from competitive sports', *Canadian Pharmacists Journal/Revue des Pharmaciens du Canada*, vol. 148, no. 4, pp.176-179.

9	Melman, S, Ashby, SE & James, C 2016, 'Supervision in practice education and transition to practice: Student and new graduate perceptions,' *Internet Journal of Allied Health Sciences and Practice*, vol. 14, no.3, p.1.

10	Bacopanos, E & Edgar, S 2016, 'Identifying the factors that affect the job satisfaction of early career Notre Dame graduate physiotherapists', *Australian Health Review*, vol. 40, no. 5, pp. 538-543.

11   Pierce, JL & Gardner, DG 2004, 'Self-esteem within the work and organizational context: A review of the organization-based self-esteem literature', *Journal of Management*, vol. 30, no. 5, pp. 591-622.

12   Orth, U 2017, 'The lifespan development of self-esteem', in *Personality Development across the Lifespan*, Specht, J, Academic Press, pp. 181-195.

13   Orth, U, Maes, J & Schmitt, M 2015, 'Self-esteem development across the life span: A longitudinal study with a large sample from Germany', *Developmental Psychology*, vol. 51, no. 2, p. 248.

14   *Definition of confidence* n.d, Merriam-Webster Dictionary, viewed 1 July 2019, https://www.merriam-webster.com/dictionary/confidence.

15   *Code of conduct for registered health practitioners* 2014, Physiotherapy Board of Australia, viewed 1 July 2019, https://www.physiotherapyboard.gov.au/Codes-Guidelines/Code-of-conduct.aspx.

16   *Code of members' professional values and behaviour* n.d, Chartered Society of Physiotherapy, viewed 27 July 2019, https://www.csp.org.uk/system/files/csp_code_of_professional_values_behaviour_full.pdf.

17   Engel, RM, Brown, BT, Swain, MS & Lystad, RP 2014, 'The provision of chiropractic, physiotherapy and osteopathic services within the Australian private health-care system: A report of recent trends', *Chiropractic & Manual Therapies*, vol. 22, no. 1, p. 3.

18   Wong, CK, Abraham, T, Karimi, P & Ow-Wing, C 2014, 'Strain counterstrain technique to decrease tender point palpation pain compared to control conditions: A systematic review with meta-analysis', *Journal of Bodywork and Movement Therapies*, vol. 18, no. 2, pp. 165-173.

19   Shah, SGS & Farrow, A 2012, 'Trends in the availability and usage of electrophysical agents in physiotherapy practices from 1990 to 2010: A review', *Physical Therapy Reviews*, vol. 17, no. 4, pp. 207-226.

20   Van Middelkoop, M, Rubinstein, SM, Kuijpers, T, Verhagen, AP, Ostelo, R, Koes, BW & van Tulder, MW 2011, 'A systematic review on the effectiveness of physical and rehabilitation interventions for chronic non-specific low back pain, *European Spine Journal*, vol. 20, no. 1, pp. 19-39.

21   Britt, H, Miller, GC, Charles, J, Henderson, J, Bayram, C, Pan, Y, Valenti, L, Harrison, C, O'Halloran, J and Fahridin, S 2010, 'General practice activity in Australia 2009–10', *General Practice Series*, vol. 27.

22   Parsons, J, Mathieson, S & Parsons, M 2015, 'Home care: An opportunity for physiotherapy', *New Zealand Journal Physiotherapy*, vol. 43, pp. 24-31.

23   Pountney, T 2007, *Physiotherapy for Children*, Elsevier Health Sciences.

24   Campos, C, Duck, M, McQuillan, R, Brazill, L, Malik, S, Hartman, L, McPherson, AC, Gibson, BE & Jachyra, P 2019, 'Exploring the role of physiotherapists in the care of children with autism spectrum disorder', *Physical & Occupational Therapy in Pediatrics*, pp. 1-15.

25   South Australia Department for Education 2017, *Legislative changes to child safe environments*, viewed 5 June 2019, https://www.education.sa.gov.au/supporting-students/child-protection/child-safe-environments/legislative-changes-child-safe-environments.

26   Government of South Australia 2019, *New working with children check*, Department of Human Services, viewed 27 July 2019, https://screening.sa.gov.au/types-of-check/new-working-with-children-checks.

27   Mistry, K, Yonezawa, E & Milne, N 2019, 'Paediatric physiotherapy curriculum: An audit and survey of Australian entry-level physiotherapy programs', *BMC Medical Education*, vol. 19, no. 1, p. 109.

28   Australian Physiotherapy Association, n.d, *Physiotherapy Vocational Rehabilitation*, viewed 3 July 2019, https://bspc.com.au/apacd/infosheet/d25.htm.

29   Frawley, HC, Neumann, P & Delany, C 2018, An argument for competency-based training in pelvic floor physiotherapy practice', *Physiotherapy Theory and Practice*, pp. 1-14.

30   Wenke, R & Mickan, S 2016, 'The role and impact of research positions within health care settings in allied health: A systematic review', *BMC Health Services Research*, vol. 16, no.1, p. 355.

31   Hurst, KM 2010, 'Experiences of new physiotherapy lecturers making the shift from clinical practice into academia', *Physiotherapy*, vol. 96, no. 3, pp. 240-247.

32   Campbell, N, McAllister, L & Eley, D 2012, 'The influence of motivation in recruitment and retention of rural and remote allied health professionals: A literature review', *Rural & Remote Health*, vol. 12, no. 3.

33   Wassinger, K & Baxter, GD 2011, 'Business plans in physiotherapy: A practical guide to writing a business plan for the non specialist', *Physical Therapy Reviews*, vol. 16, no.3, pp. 210-211.

34   Castin, M 2019, 'Non-clinical jobs for physiotherapists', *The Non-Clinical PT*, viewed 3 March 2019, https://thenonclinicalpt.com/non-clinical-jobs-physical-therapists.

35   French, HP & Dowds, J 2008, 'An overview of continuing professional development in physiotherapy', *Physiotherapy*, vol. 94, no. 3, pp. 190-197.

36   D'Souza, J & Gurin, M 2016, 'The universal significance of Maslow's concept of self-actualisation', *The Humanistic Psychologist*, vol. 44, no.2, pp. 210.

37   McLeod, S 2007, 'Maslow's hierarchy of needs', *Simply Psychology*, vol. 1.

38   Chipchase, LS, Johnston, V & Long, PD 2012, 'Continuing professional development: The missing link', *Manual Therapy*, vol. 17, no.1, pp. 89-91.

39   *Physiotherapy Career Pathway: White Paper* 2016, Australian Physiotherapy Association, viewed 7 May 2019, https://australian.physio/sites/default/files/professional-development/download/career-pathway/WhitePaper_APACareerPathway.pdf.

40   Mathur, S 2011, 'Doctorate in physical therapy: Is it time for a conversation?', *Physiotherapy Canada*, vol. 63, no. 2, pp.140-142.

41   *Your Career Pathway* 2017, Australian Physiotherapy Association, viewed 6 June 2019, https://www.physiotherapy.asn.au/APAWCM/Careers/Career_Paths/Titling.aspx.

42   Maslach, C, Schaufeli, WB & Leiter, MP 2001, 'Job burnout', *Annual Review of Psychology*, vol. 52, no.1, pp. 397-422.

43   Johnston, C, Luscombe, D & Fordham, L 2016, 'Working with families as part of early childhood intervention services', *Early Childhood Intervention: Working with Families of Young Children with Special Needs*, pp. 129.

44   Tasker, D, Loftus, S & Higgs, J 2012, 'Head, heart and hands: Creating mindful dialogues in community-based physiotherapy', *New Zealand Journal of Physiotherapy*, vol. 40, no. 1, pp. 5.

45   Singla, M, Jones, M, Edwards, I & Kumar, S 2015, 'Physiotherapists' assessment of patients' psychosocial status: Are we standing on thin ice? A qualitative descriptive study', *Manual Therapy*, vol. 20, no.2, pp. 328-334.

46   Wilson, D, Williams, M & Butler, D 2009, 'Language and the pain experience', *Physiotherapy Research International*, vol. 14, no.1, pp. 56-65.

47   Ezzat, AM & Maly, MR 2012, 'Building passion develops meaningful mentoring relationships among Canadian physiotherapists', *Physiotherapy Canada*, vol. 64, no.1, pp. 77-85.

48   Davies, JM, Edgar, S & Debenham, J 2016, 'A qualitative exploration of the factors influencing the job satisfaction and career development of physiotherapists in private practice', *Manual Therapy*, vol. 25, pp. 56-61.

49   Stewart, S & Carpenter, C 2009, 'Electronic mentoring: An innovative approach to providing clinical support', *International Journal of Therapy and Rehabilitation*, vol. 16, no. 4, pp. 199-206.

50   De Dreu, CK 2015, 'Conflict and conflict management', *Wiley Encyclopedia of Management*, pp. 1-4.

51   Proksch, S 2016, *Conflict Management*, Springer.

52   Einarsen, S, Skogstad, A, Rørvik, E, Lande, ÅB & Nielsen, MB 2018, 'Climate for conflict management, exposure to workplace bullying and work engagement: A moderated mediation analysis', *The International Journal of Human Resource Management*, vol. 29, no. 3, pp. 549-570.

53   Kang, M & Sung, M 2017, 'How symmetrical employee communication leads to employee engagement and positive employee communication behaviors: The mediation of employee-organization relationships', *Journal of Communication Management*, vol. 21, no. 1, pp. 82-102.

54   Reeves, S, Perrier, L, Goldman, J, Freeth, D & Zwarenstein, M 2013, 'Interprofessional education: Effects on professional practice and healthcare outcomes', *Cochrane Database of Systematic Reviews*, vol. 3.

55   Olson, R & Bialocerkowski, A 2014, 'Interprofessional education in allied health: A systematic review', *Medical Education*, vol. 48, no. 3, pp. 236-246.

56   Gilliland, S & Wainwright, SF 2017, 'Patterns of clinical reasoning in physical therapist students', *Physical Therapy*, vol. 97, no. 5, pp. 499-511.

57   Chaffey, L, Unsworth, C & Fossey, E, 2010, 'A grounded theory of intuition among occupational therapists in mental health practice', *British Journal of Occupational Therapy*, vol. 73, no. 7, pp. 300-308.

58   Holdar, U, Wallin, L & Heiwe, S 2013, 'Why do we do as we do? Factors influencing clinical reasoning and decision-making among physiotherapists in an acute setting', *Physiotherapy Research International*, vol. 18, no. 4, pp. 220-229.

59   Scurlock-Evans, L, Upton, P & Upton, D 2014, 'Evidence-based practice in physiotherapy: A systematic review of barriers, enablers and interventions', *Physiotherapy*, vol. 100, no. 3, pp. 208-219.

60   Elkins, MR, Moseley, AM, Sherrington, C, Herbert, RD & Maher, CG 2013, 'Growth in the Physiotherapy Evidence Database (PEDro) and

use of the PEDro scale, *British Journal of Sports Medicine*, vol. 47, no. 4, pp. 188-189.

61   McEvoy, MP, Williams, MT, Olds, TS, Lewis, LK & Petkov, J 2011, 'Evidence-based practice profiles of physiotherapists transitioning into the workforce: A study of two cohorts', *BMC Medical Education*, vol. 11, no. 1, p. 100.

62   Wedge, FM, Braswell-Christy, J, Brown, CJ, Foley, KT, Graham, C & Shaw, S 2012, 'Factors influencing the use of outcome measures in physical therapy practice', *Physiotherapy Theory and Practice*, vol. 28, no. 2, pp. 119-133.

63   Sackett, DL, Straus, SE, Richardson, SW, Rosenberg, W, Haynes & BR 2000, *Evidence-based Medicine*, 2nd edn, London: Churchill Livingstone.

64   *Standards for Physiotherapy Practices* 2011, Australian Physiotherapy Association, viewed 4 May 2019, https://australian.physio/sites/default/files/tools/Resources_Private_Practice_Standards_for_physiotherapy_practices_2011.pdf.

65   Pedersen, TJ & Kristensen, HK 2016, 'A critical discourse analysis of the attitudes of occupational therapists and physiotherapists towards the systematic use of standardised outcome measurement', *Disability and Rehabilitation*, vol. 38, no. 16, pp. 1592-1602.

66   *Work Health and Safety Act* 2012, Government of South Australia, viewed 6 July 2019. https://www.legislation.sa.gov.au/LZ/C/A/WORK%20HEALTH%20AND%20SAFETY%20ACT%202012.aspx.

67   *WHS compliance, injury reporting, licensing and compensation claims* 2019, Safe Work Australia. viewed 5 July 2019, https://www.safeworkaustralia.gov.au.

68   *Guidelines for claiming workers compensation* 2019, State Insurance Regulatory Authority New South Wales Government, viewed 4 July 2019, https://www.sira.nsw.gov.au/resources-library/workers-compensation-resources/publications/workers-compensation-policies/Guidelines-for-claiming-workers-compensation-8084.pdf.

69   *Physiotherapy Services Policy* 2019, WorkSafe Victoria, viewed 5 July 2019, https://www.worksafe.vic.gov.au/physiotherapy-services-policy.

70   Daly, A 2016, 'Worklessness: Can physiotherapists do more?', *Journal of Physiotherapy*, vol. 62, no. 4, pp. 179-180.

71   *State Insurance Regulatory Authority Independent Consultants* 2019, New South Wales Government, viewed 5 July 2019, https://www.sira.nsw.gov.au/for-service-providers/A-Z-of-service-providers/independent-consultants.

72   Elbers, NA, Akkermans, AJ, Lockwood, K, Craig, A & Cameron, ID 2015, 'Factors that challenge health for people involved in the compensation process following a motor vehicle crash: A longitudinal study', *BMC Public Health*, vol. 15, no. 1, p. 339.

73   D'Souza, F, Egan, SJ & Rees, CS 2011, 'The relationship between perfectionism, stress and burnout in clinical psychologists', *Behaviour Change*, vol. 28, no. 1, pp. 17-28.

74   Craiovan, PM 2014, 'Correlations between perfectionism, stress, psychopathological symptoms and burnout in the medical field', *Procedia-Social and Behavioral Sciences*, vol. 127, pp. 529-533.

75   Silverman, LK 2007, 'Perfectionism: The crucible of giftedness', *Gifted Education International*, vol. 23, no. 3, pp. 233-245.

76   Hendlin, SJ 1992, *When Good Enough is Never Enough: Escaping the Perfection Trap*, JP Tarcher

77   Greenspon, TS 1999, 'Perfectionism is not healthy', *Annual Meeting of the National Association for Gifted Children*, Albuquerque, NM.

78   Irving, JA, Dobkin, PL & Park, J 2009, 'Cultivating mindfulness in health care professionals: A review of empirical studies of mindfulness-based stress reduction (MBSR)', *Complementary Therapies in Clinical Practice*, vol. 15, no. 2, pp. 61-66.

79   *Definition of overcommitment*, n.d, Merriam-Webster Dictionary, viewed 1 July 2019, https://www.merriam-webster.com/dictionary/overcommit.

80   Lang, J, Kern, M & Zapf, D 2016, 'Retaining high achievers in times of demographic change: The effects of proactivity, career satisfaction and job embeddedness on voluntary turnover', *Psychology*, vol. 7, no. 13, pp. 1545.

81   Skovholt, TM & Trotter-Mathison, M 2014, *The Resilient Practitioner: Burnout Prevention and Self-care Strategies for Counselors, Therapists, Teachers, and Health Professionals*, Routledge.

82   Russell, R 2017, 'On overcoming imposter syndrome', *Academic Medicine*, vol. 92, no. 8, pp. 1070.

83   Clance, PR, Dingman, D, Reviere, SL & Stober, DR 1995, 'Impostor phenomenon in an interpersonal/social context: Origins and treatment', *Women & Therapy*, vol. 16, no. 4, pp. 79-96.

84   Friedman, M 1974, *Treating Type A Behavior and Your Heart*, Fawceff Crest.

85   Ryckman, RM, Hammer, M, Kaczor, LM & Gold, JA 1990, 'Construction of a hypercompetitive attitude scale', *Journal of Personality Assessment*, vol. 55, no. 3-4, pp. 630-639.

86   Okoro, CM, Okonkwo, EA, Eze, AC, Chigbo, CM & Nwandu, IB 2018, 'Competitiveness among employees in the workplace: The influence of conflict handling styles and organisational types', *IOSR Journal of Humanities and Social Science*, vol. 23, no. 6, pp. 82-89.

87   Cooper, I & Jenkins, S 2008, 'Sexual boundaries between physiotherapists and patients are not perceived clearly: An observational study', *Australian Journal of Physiotherapy*, vol. 54, no. 4, pp. 275-279.

88   Basevi, R, Reid, D & Godbold, R 2014, 'Ethical guidelines and the use of social media and text messaging in health care: A review of literature', *New Zealand Journal of Physiotherapy*, vol. 42, no. 2, pp. 68-80.

89   Simpson, JK 2019, 'At-risk advertising by Australian chiropractors and physiotherapists', *Chiropractic & Manual Therapies*, vol. 27, no. 1, pp. 30.

90   Muller, MD, Moyes, SA & Fulcher, ML 2016, 'Text messaging between clinicians and patients – Hve we got thngs unda cntrl?', *Journal of Primary Health Care*, vol. 8, no. 4, pp. 351-356.

91   Delany, C 2007, 'In private practice, informed consent is interpreted as providing explanations rather than offering choices: A qualitative study', *Australian Journal of Physiotherapy*, vol. 53, no. 3, pp. 171-177.

92   Magarey, ME, Rebbeck, T, Coughlan, B, Grimmer, K, Rivett, DA & Refshauge, K 2004, 'Pre-manipulative testing of the cervical spine review, revision and new clinical guidelines', *Manual Therapy*, vol. 9, no. 2, pp. 95-108.

93   Thomas, L, Shirley, D, Rivett, D 2006, 'Clinical guide to safe manual therapy practice in the cervical spine', Australian Physiotherapy Association, viewed 1 July 2019, https://australian.physio/tools/clinical-practice/cervical-spine.

94   Brazier, M 1992, *Medicine, Patients and the Law*, 2nd edn, Harmondsworth: Penguin Books.

95   *Patient Examination Guidelines* 2012, Australian Medical Association, viewed 22 July 2019, https://ama.com.au/sites/default/files/documents/Patient_Examination_Guidelines_2012_0.pdf.

96   *Guidelines for allied health assistants documenting in health records* 2016, Allied Health Professions' Office of Queensland, viewed 20 July 2019 https://www.health.qld.gov.au/__data/assets/pdf_file/0029/144866/ahadocguide.pdf.

97   Olawale, OA, Akodu, AK & Tabeson, EA 2015, 'Analysis of physiotherapy documentation of patients' records and discharge plans in a tertiary hospital', *Journal of Clinical Sciences*, vol. 12, no. 2, p. 85.

98   Phillips, A, Stiller, K & Williams, M 2006, 'Medical record documentation: The quality of physiotherapy entries', *Internet Journal of Allied Health Sciences and Practice*, vol. 4, no. 3, p. 4.

99   *My Health Record* 2019, Australian Government Australian Digital Health Agency, viewed 1 July 2019 https://www.myhealthrecord.gov.au/.

100   Walsh, L, Hemsley, B, Allan, M, Adams, N, Balandin, S, Georgiou, A, Higgins, I, McCarthy, S & Hill, S 2017, 'The e-health literacy demands of Australia's My Health Record: A heuristic evaluation of usability', *Perspectives in Health Information Management*, vol. 14.

101   *The Flag System*, 2018, Physiopedia, viewed 20 July https://www.physio-pedia.com/index.php?title=The_Flag_System&oldid=197829.

102   *Physiotherapist Salaries in Australia* 2019, Indeed, viewed 20 July 2019, https://au.indeed.com/salaries/Physiotherapist-Salaries?period=HOURLY.

103   *Average Physiotherapist Salary in Australia* 2019, Payscale, viewed 20 July 2019, https://www.payscale.com/research/AU/Job=Physiotherapist/Salary.

104   Szuster, F & Carson, E 2007, 'Career study of South Australian medical, dental and physiotherapy graduates', Adelaide, Australia: South Australian Department of Health.

105   *Pay Guide – Health Professionals and Support Services Award* 2010, Fair Work Ombudsman, viewed 3 July 2019, https://www.fairwork.gov.au/ArticleDocuments/872/health-professionals-and-support-services-award-ma000027-pay-guide.pdf.aspx.

106   Keller, G, Papasan, J 2013, *The One Thing: The Surprisingly Simple Truth Behind Extraordinary Results*, Hachette UK.

107   Klappa, SG, Fulton, LE, Cerier, L, Peña, A, Sibenaller, A & Klappa, SP 2015, 'Compassion fatigue among physiotherapist and physical therapists around the world', *Health Education*, vol. 3, no.5, pp. 124-137.

108   *Paid Parental Leave Evaluation* 2014, The University of Queensland Australia, viewed 28 July 2019, https://www.dss.gov.au/sites/default/files/documents/03_2015/finalphase4_report_6_march_2015_0.pdf.

109   *Australian Institute of Family Studies* 2018, viewed 3 June 2019, https://aifs.gov.au/facts-and-figures/births-australia.

110   Alonso, J, Petukhova, M, Vilagut, G, Chatterji, S, Heeringa, S, Üstün, TB, Alhamzawi, AO, Viana, MC, Angermeyer, M, Bromet, E & Bruffaerts, R 2011, 'Days out of role due to common physical and mental conditions: Results from the WHO World Mental Health surveys', *Molecular Psychiatry*, vol. 16, no. 12, pp. 1234.

111 Breen, LJ, O'Connor, M, Hewitt, LY & Lobb, EA 2014, 'The "specter" of cancer: Exploring secondary trauma for health professionals providing cancer support and counseling', *Psychological Services*, vol. 11, no. 1, p. 60.

112 Bandini, J 2015, 'The medicalisation of bereavement:(Ab)normal grief in the DSM-5', *Death Studies*, vol. 39, no. 6, pp. 347-352.

113 Scutter, S & Goold, M 1995, 'Burnout in recently qualified physiotherapists in South Australia', *Australian Journal of Physiotherapy*, vol. 41, no. 2, pp. 115-118.

114 Maslach, C, Jackson, SE & Leiter, MP 1996, *Burnout Inventory Manual*, Palo Alto, California Consulting Psychological Press.

115 Ben-Zur, H 2019, 'Transactional Model of Stress and Coping', *Encyclopedia of Personality and Individual Differences*, pp.1-4.

116 Staal, MA 2004, *Stress, cognition, and human performance: A literature review and conceptual framework*, Ames Research Center, Moflett Field, California.

117 Cañadas-De la Fuente, GA, Vargas, C, San Luis, C, García, I, Cañadas, G.R & Emilia, I 2015, 'Risk factors and prevalence of burnout syndrome in the nursing profession', *International Journal of Nursing Studies*, vol. 52, no. 1, pp. 240-249.

118 Rotenstein, LS, Torre, M, Ramos, MA, Rosales, RC, Guille, C, Sen, S & Mata, DA 2018, 'Prevalence of burnout among physicians: A systematic review', *Jama*, vol. 320, no. 11, pp. 1131-1150.

119 McCormack, HM, MacIntyre, TE, O'Shea, D, Herring, MP & Campbell, MJ 2018, 'The prevalence and cause(s) of burnout among applied psychologists: A systematic review', *Frontiers in Psychology*, vol. 9.

120 Śliwiński, Z, Starczyńska, M, Kotela, I, Kowalski, T, Kryś-Noszczyk, K, Lietz-Kijak, D, Kijak, E & Makara-Studzińska, M 2014, 'Life satisfaction and risk of burnout among men and women working as physiotherapists', *International Journal of Occupational Medicine and Environmental Health*, vol. 27, no. 3, pp. 400-412.

121 Klappa, SG, Howayek, R, Reed, K, Scherbarth, B & Klappa, SP 2015, 'Compassion fatigue among new graduate physical therapists', *Education*, vol. 3, no. 4, pp. 100-111.

122 Wilski, M, Chmielewski, B & Tomczak, M 2015, 'Work locus of control and burnout in Polish physiotherapists: The mediating effect of coping styles', *International Journal of Occupational Medicine and Environmental Health*, vol. 28, no. 5, pp. 875.

123   Shin, H, Park, YM, Ying, JY, Kim, B, Noh, H & Lee, SM 2014, 'Relationships between coping strategies and burnout symptoms: A meta-analytic approach', *Professional Psychology: Research and Practice*, vol. 45, no. 1, pp. 44-55.

124   Polman, R, Borkoles, E & Nicholls, AR 2010, 'Type D personality, stress, and symptoms of burnout: The influence of avoidance coping and social support', *British Journal of Health Psychology*, vol. 15, no. 3, pp. 681-696.

125   Westman, M & Bakker, AB 2008, 'Crossover of burnout among health care professionals', *Stress and Burnout in Health Care*, pp. 111-125.

126   Edelwich, J & Brodsky, A 1980, 'Burn-out: Stages of disillusionment in the helping professions', *New York: Human Sciences Press*, vol. 1.

127   Bourg Carter, S 2013, 'The tell-tale signs of burnout, do you have them?', *Psychology Today*, pp. 498-512.

128   Śliwiński, Z, Starczyńska, M, Kotela, I, Kowalski, T, Kryś-Noszczyk, K, Lietz-Kijak, D, Kijak, E and Makara-Studzińska, M, 2014, 'Burnout among physiotherapists and length of service', *International Journal of Occupational Medicine and Environmental Health*, vol. 27, no. 2, pp. 224-235.

129   Adegoke, BO, Akodu, AK & Oyeyemi, AL 2008, 'Work-related musculoskeletal disorders among Nigerian physiotherapists', *BMC Musculoskeletal Disorders*, vol. 9, no. 1, p. 112.

130   Corrado, B, Ciardi, G, Fortunato, L & Servodio Iammarrone, C 2018, 'Burnout syndrome among Italian physiotherapists: A cross-sectional study', *European Journal of Physiotherapy*, pp. 1-6.

131   Kerckhofs, E & Van Campenhout, J 2015, 'Burnout in physiotherapists working in Flemish rehabilitation centres', *Physiotherapy*, vol. 101, pp. 739-740.

132   Seixas, A, Marques, T, Moreira-Silva, I, Azevedo, J & Rodrigues, S 2019, 'The prevalence of burnout in Portuguese physiotherapists', *Occupational and Environmental Safety and Health*, pp. 591-600.

133   Darragh, AR, Huddleston, W & King, P 2009, 'Work-related musculoskeletal injuries and disorders among occupational and physical therapists', *American Journal of Occupational Therapy*, vol. 63, no. 3, pp. 351-362.

134   Nordin, NAM, Leonard, JH & Thye, NC 2011, 'Work-related injuries among physiotherapists in public hospitals: A Southeast Asian picture', *Clinics*, vol. 66, no. 3, pp. 373-378.

135   Cromie, JE, Robertson, VJ & Best, MO 2000, 'Work-related musculoskeletal disorders in physical therapists: Prevalence, severity, risks, and responses', *Physical Therapy*, vol. 80, no. 4, pp. 336-351.

136	Passier, L & McPhail, S 2011, 'Work related musculoskeletal disorders amongst therapists in physically demanding roles: Qualitative analysis of risk factors and strategies for prevention', *BMC Musculoskeletal Disorders*, vol. 12, no.1, pp. 24.

137	Buckle, PW & Devereux, JJ 2002, 'The nature of work-related neck and upper limb musculoskeletal disorders', *Applied Ergonomics*, vol. 33, no. 3, pp. 207-217.

138	Glover, W 2003, 'Lifting the lid on work-related ill-health and musculoskeletal injury: CSP embarks on large-scale member study' *Physiotherapy Journal*, vol. 89, no. 7, pp. 394-395.

139	McPhail, SM & Waite, MC 2014, 'Physical activity and health-related quality of life among physiotherapists: A cross sectional survey in an Australian hospital and health service', *Journal of Occupational Medicine and Toxicology*, vol. 9, no. 1, p. 1.

140	McMeeken, J, Grant, R, Webb, G, Krause, KL & Garnett, R 2008, 'Australian physiotherapy student intake is increasing and attrition remains lower than the university average: A demographic study', *Australian Journal of Physiotherapy*, vol. 54, no. 1, pp. 65-71.

141	Mitchell, M 2019, 'Enabling overseas physiotherapists to fill the void', *InMotion*, February edn, pp. 32-38.

142	Mulcahy, AJ, Jones, S, Strauss, G & Cooper, I 2010, 'The impact of recent physiotherapy graduates in the workforce: A study of Curtin University entry-level physiotherapists 2000–2004', *Australian Health Review*, vol. 34, no. 2, pp. 252-259.

143	Macdonald, JL & Levy, SR 2016, 'Ageism in the workplace: The role of psychosocial factors in predicting job satisfaction, commitment, and engagement', *Journal of Social Issues*, vol. 72, no. 1, pp. 169-190.

144	Śliwiński, Z, Starczynská, M, Kotela, I, Kowalski, T, Kryś-Noszczyk, K, Lietz-Kijak, D, Kijak, E. & Makara-Studzinska, M 2014, 'Burnout among physiotherapists and length of service', *International Journal of Occupational Medicine and Environmental Health*, vol. 27, no. 2, pp. 224-235.

145	*Position statement: Scope of practice* 2009, Australian Physiotherapy Association, viewed 1 July 2019, https://australian.physio/sites/default/files/RESOURCES/Advocacy_Position_Scope_of_Practice_2009.pdf.

146	*WA Health expanded scope of practice physiotherapy project* 2015, Government of Western Australia Department of Health, viewed 3 July 2019, https://ww2.health.wa.gov.au/~/media/Files/Corporate/general%20documents/Chief%20Health%20Professions%20Office/PDF/WA-Health-Physiotherapy-Expanded-Scope-of-Practice-Project-A-Literature-Overview-2015.pdf.

147   Stanhope, J, Grimmer-Somers, K, Milanese, S, Kumar, S & Morris, J 2012, 'Extended scope physiotherapy roles for orthopedic outpatients: An update systematic review of the literature', *Journal of Multidisciplinary Healthcare*, vol. 5, p.37.

148   Padilla-Castañeda, M.A, Sotgiu, E, Barsotti, M, Frisoli, A, Orsini, P, Martiradonna, A, Laddaga, C & Bergamasco, M 2018, 'An orthopaedic robotic-assisted rehabilitation method of the forearm in virtual reality physiotherapy', *Journal of Healthcare Engineering*, vol 2018, p. 1-20.

149   Yelvar, G.D.Y, Çırak, Y, Dalkılınç, M, Demir, Y.P, Guner, Z & Boydak, A 2017, 'Is physiotherapy integrated virtual walking effective on pain, function, and kinesiophobia in patients with non-specific low-back pain? Randomised controlled trial', *European Spine Journal*, vol. 26, no. 2, pp. 538-545.

150   Laver, K, George, S, Ratcliffe, J, Quinn, S, Whitehead, C, Davies, O & Crotty, M 2012, 'Use of an interactive video gaming program compared with conventional physiotherapy for hospitalised older adults: A feasibility trial', *Disability and Rehabilitation*, vol. 32, no. 21, pp. 1802-1808.

151   Ferrarin, M, Rabuffetti, M, Bacchini, M, Casiraghi, A, Castagna, A, Pizzi, A & Montesano, A 2015, 'Does gait analysis change clinical decision-making in post-stroke patients? Results from a pragmatic prospective observational study', *European Journal Physical Rehabilitation Medicine*, vol. 51, no. 2, pp. 171-84.

152   Wright, A, Moss, P, Dennis, DM, Harrold, M, Levy, S, Furness, AL & Reubenson, A 2018, 'The influence of a full-time, immersive simulation-based clinical placement on physiotherapy student confidence during the transition to clinical practice', *Advances in Simulation*, vol. 3, no. 1, p. 3.

153   O'Sullivan, PB, Caneiro, JP, O'Keeffe, M, Smith, A, Dankaerts, W, Fersum, K & O'Sullivan, K 2018, 'Cognitive functional therapy: An integrated behavioral approach for the targeted management of disabling low back pain', *Physical Therapy*, vol. 98, no. 5, pp. 408-423.

154   Bunzli, S, Smith, A, Schütze, R & O'Sullivan, P 2015, 'Beliefs underlying pain-related fear and how they evolve: A qualitative investigation in people with chronic back pain and high pain-related fear', *BMJ Open*, vol. 5, no. 10.

155   Schoeb, V, Staffoni, L, Parry, R & Pilnick, A 2014, 'What do you expect from physiotherapy? A detailed analysis of goal setting in physiotherapy.' *Disability and Rehabilitation*, vol. 36, no. 20, pp. 1679-1686.

156   *Physical activity and adults*, 2019, World Health Organization, viewed 10 July 2019, https://www.who.int/dietphysicalactivity/factsheet_adults/en/.

157   Morgan, F, Battersby, A, Weightman, AL, Searchfield, L, Turley, R, Morgan, H, Jagroo, J & Ellis, S 2016, 'Adherence to exercise referral schemes by participants – What do providers and commissioners need to know? A systematic review of barriers and facilitators', *BMC Public Health*, vol. 16, no. 1, pp. 227.

158   Bachmann, C, Oesch, P & Bachmann, S 2018, 'Recommendations for improving adherence to home-based exercise: A systematic review', *Physikalische Medizin, Rehabilitationsmedizin, Kurortmedizin*, vol. 28, no, 1, pp. 20-31.

159   Jack, K, McLean, SM, Moffett, JK & Gardiner, E 2010, 'Barriers to treatment adherence in physiotherapy outpatient clinics: A systematic review', *Manual Therapy*, vol. 15, no. 3, pp. 220-228.

160   Wade, DT & Halligan, PW 2017, 'The biopsychosocial model of illness: A model whose time has come', *Clinical Rehabilitation*, vol. 31, no. 8, pp. 995-1004.

161   Houben, M & Moermans, I 2014, 'What is the importance of holistic therapy for physical therapists?', Master's thesis, UHasselt.

162   Grace Stineman, M 2011, 'The clinician's voice of brain and heart: A biopsycho-ecological framework for merging the biomedical and holistic', *Topics in Stroke Rehabilitation*, vol. 18, no. 1, pp. 55-59.

163   García-Escamilla, E, Rodríguez-Martín, B & Martínez-Vizcaíno, V 2016, 'Integration of acupuncture into conventional medicine from health professionals' perspective: A thematic synthesis of qualitative studies', *Health*, vol. 20, no. 2, pp. 176-200.

164   Hopton, AK, Curnoe, S, Kanaan, M & MacPherson, H 2012, 'Acupuncture in practice: Mapping the providers, the patients and the settings in a national cross-sectional survey', *BMJ Open*, vol. 2, no. 1.

165   Dunning, J, Butts, R, Mourad, F, Young, I, Flannagan, S & Perreault, T 2014, 'Dry needling: A literature review with implications for clinical practice guidelines', *Physical Therapy Reviews*, vol. 19, no. 4, pp. 252-265.

166   Chon, TY & Lee, MC 2013, 'Acupuncture', *Mayo Clinic Proceedings*, vol. 88, no. 10, pp. 1141-1146.

167   Li, QQ, Shi, GX, Xu, Q, Wang, J, Liu, CZ & Wang, LP 2013, 'Acupuncture effect and central autonomic regulation', *Evidence-Based Complementary and Alternative Medicine*, p. 1-6.

168   Aveni, E, Bauer, B, Ramelet, AS, Kottelat, Y, Decosterd, I, Finti, G, Ballabeni, P, Bonvin, E & Rodondi, PY 2016, 'The attitudes of physicians, nurses, physical therapists, and midwives toward complementary medicine

for chronic pain: A survey at an academic hospital', *Explore*, vol. 12, no. 5, pp. 341-346.

169   Adams, J, Lui, CW, Sibbritt, D, Broom, A, Wardle, J & Homer, C 2011, 'Attitudes and referral practices of maternity care professionals with regard to complementary and alternative medicine: An integrative review', *Journal of Advanced Nursing*, vol. 67, no. 3, pp. 472-483.

170   Leach, MJ & Steel, A 2018, 'The potential downstream effects of proposed changes in Australian private health insurance policy: The case for naturopathy', *Advances in Integrative Medicine*, vol. 5, no. 2, pp. 48-51.

171   Hughes, CM, Quinn, F & Baxter, GD 2011, 'Complementary and alternative medicine: Perception and use by physiotherapists in the management of low back pain', *Complementary Therapies in Medicine*, vol. 19, no. 3, pp. 149-154.

172   *Defintion of mindfulness*, n.d, Merriam-Webster Dictionary, viewed 28 July 2019 https://www.merriam-webster.com/dictionary/mindfulness.

173   Tasker, D, Loftus, S & Higgs, J 2012, 'Head, heart and hands: Creating mindful dialogues in community-based physiotherapy', *New Zealand Journal of Physiotherapy*, vol. 40, no. 1, pp. 5.

174   Aburn, G, Gott, M & Hoare, K 2016, 'What is resilience? An integrative review of the empirical literature', *Journal of Advanced Nursing*, vol. 72, no. 5, pp. 980-1000.

175   Delany, C, Miller, KJ, El-Ansary, D, Remedios, L, Hosseini, A & McLeod, S 2015, 'Replacing stressful challenges with positive coping strategies: A resilience program for clinical placement learning', *Advances in Health Sciences Education*, vol. 20, no. 5, pp. 1303-1324.

176   *Definition of thrive*, n.d, Merriam-Webster Dictionary, viewed 10 July 2019 https://www.merriam-webster.com/dictionary/thrive.

177   Strömberg, A, Jaarsma, T, & Riegel, B 2012, 'Self-care: Who cares?', *European Journal of Cardiovascular Nursing*, vol. 11, no. 2, pp. 133-134.

178   Hughes, N & Burke, J 2018, 'Sleeping with the frenemy: How restricting 'bedroom use' of smartphones impacts happiness and wellbeing', *Computers in Human Behavior*, vol. 85, pp. 236-244.

179   Maslach, C & Leiter, M.P 2017, 'New insights into burnout and health care: Strategies for improving civility and alleviating burnout', *Medical Teacher*, vol. 39, no. 2, pp. 160-163.

180   Maclean, M, Harvey, C & Gordon, J 2013, 'Social innovation, social entrepreneurship and the practice of contemporary entrepreneurial philanthropy', *International Small Business Journal*, vol. 31, no. 7, pp. 747-763.

181 Vallerand, RJ 2012, 'The role of passion in sustainable psychological well-being', *Psychology of Well-Being: Theory, Research and Practice*, vol. 2, no. 1, p. 1.

182 Maclean, M, Harvey, C & Gordon, J 2013, 'Social innovation, social entrepreneurship and the practice of contemporary entrepreneurial philanthropy', *International Small Business Journal*, vol. 31, no. 7, pp. 747-763.

www.ingramcontent.com/pod-product-compliance
Lightning Source LLC
Chambersburg PA
CBHW021107080526
44587CB00010B/419